William Turnbull
sculpture and paintings

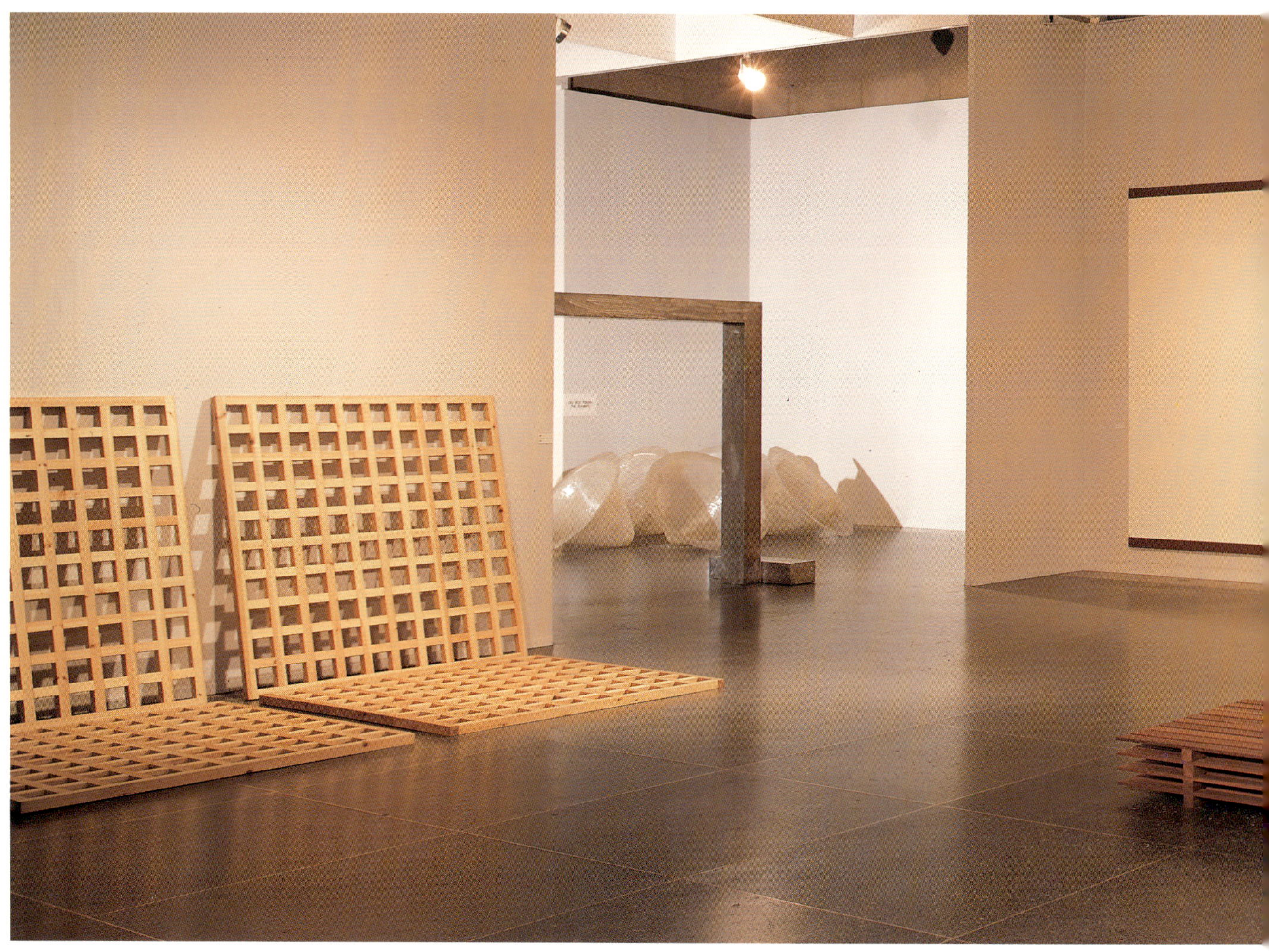

William Turnbull
sculpture and paintings

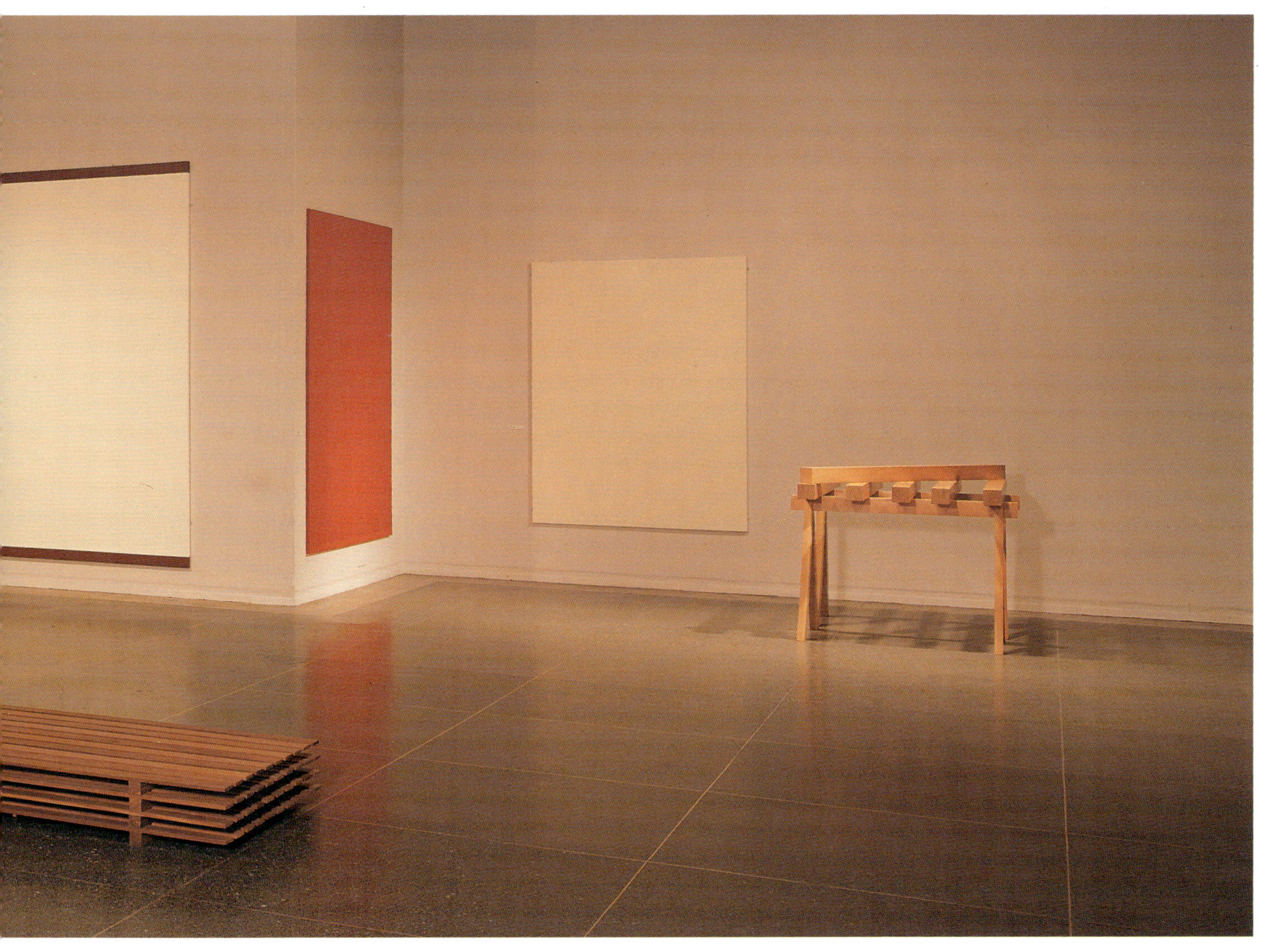

MERRELL HOLBERTON PUBLISHERS LONDON
in association with Serpentine Gallery

This book is published to accompany the exhibition, *Bronze Idols and Untitled Paintings*, curated by David Sylvester, at the Serpentine Gallery, London, 15 November 1995 – 7 January 1996

Bronze Idols and Untitled Paintings is sponsored by
TAG HEUER

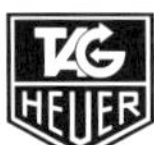

Generous assistance has also been received from THE HENRY MOORE FOUNDATION

Recent photography by Prudence Cuming Associates and Richard Thomas; black-and-white photography and photographs up to 1963 by the artist and Kim Lim

ISBN 1 85894 024 9

First published in 1995 by Merrell Holberton Publishers and the Serpentine Gallery
Produced by Merrell Holberton Publishers, Axe & Bottle Court, 70 Newcomen Street, London SE1 1YT
Designed by Roger Davies
Typeset by SX Composing, Rayleigh
Printed in England by Jarrolds

COVER *Queen 2* 1988 (plate 55)
TITLEPAGE Installation, *William Turnbull* exhibition, Tate Gallery, London, 1973

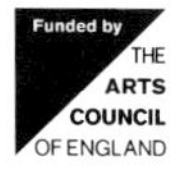 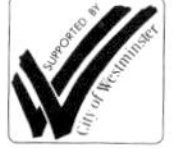

Contents

Form, Function and Design

Since 1860, the company that was founded by Edward Heuer has been inextricably linked with innovation and design. From the first chronograph in 1916, technology has determined function and function has created design.

TAG Heuer are committed sponsors at both local and international levels and sponsor some of the most technically advanced and high-profile sporting events in the world: Formula One Grand Prix, the America's Cup and the World Cup Skiing in the USA. Sport and its sponsorship are a challenging testing-ground to ensure the company stays at the forefront of watch technology. Sponsorship of the arts, we believe, is a natural and exciting extension to our sponsorship programme, consistent with our brand philosophy. At the root of TAG Heuer's style is the unique combination of technical excellence, modernity and prestige. We are creating modern classics for the twenty-first century.

Christian Viros, Chief Executive
TAG Heuer SA

TAG Heuer is proud to be sponsoring the first solo exhibition of sculpture and paintings by William Turnbull in a public space since his retrospective at the Tate Gallery in 1973.

William Turnbull is one of Britain's most established and well respected living artists and TAG Heuer is delighted to be associated with this exhibition which gives the public the opportunity to experience his innovative yet classic work.

Over the last twenty-five years the Serpentine Gallery has established a reputation for creating public debate surrounding new developments in contemporary art. This challenging approach to art and design reflects TAG Heuer's own continuing search for excellence and innovation in the fields of design and technology.

Neil Duckworth, Managing Director
TAG Heuer UK

Director's Foreword

The Serpentine is committed to presenting exhibitions by important senior British artists and we responded enthusiastically to David Sylvester's proposal to curate a show of William Turnbull's work especially for the Gallery. We agreed that while presenting a general selection of the paintings, the choice of sculpture should concentrate on groups of works which could loosely be described as 'bronze idols' and which date from two periods, the second half of the 1950s and from 1979 onwards.

Both the exhibition, 'Bronze Idols and Untitled Paintings', and this book with its notable scholarly essay by Patrick Elliott, are the first initiatives in the public domain devoted to Turnbull's work for twenty-two years. It has been a privilege and a pleasure to collaborate on both with the artist.

Tag Heuer have provided valuable assistance and we are delighted that they have chosen this exhibition as their first visual arts sponsorship. The Henry Moore Foundation pledged their help to the exhibition at an early stage and we are indebted to them for their continuing support of the Gallery.

We have worked closely with Hester van Royen at Waddington Galleries who, together with Sarah Tooley, has provided indispensable help and advice.

Finally, our warmest thanks are extended to the lenders who have generously entrusted into our care important works by the artist for the exhibition.

Julia Peyton-Jones, Director
The Serpentine Gallery

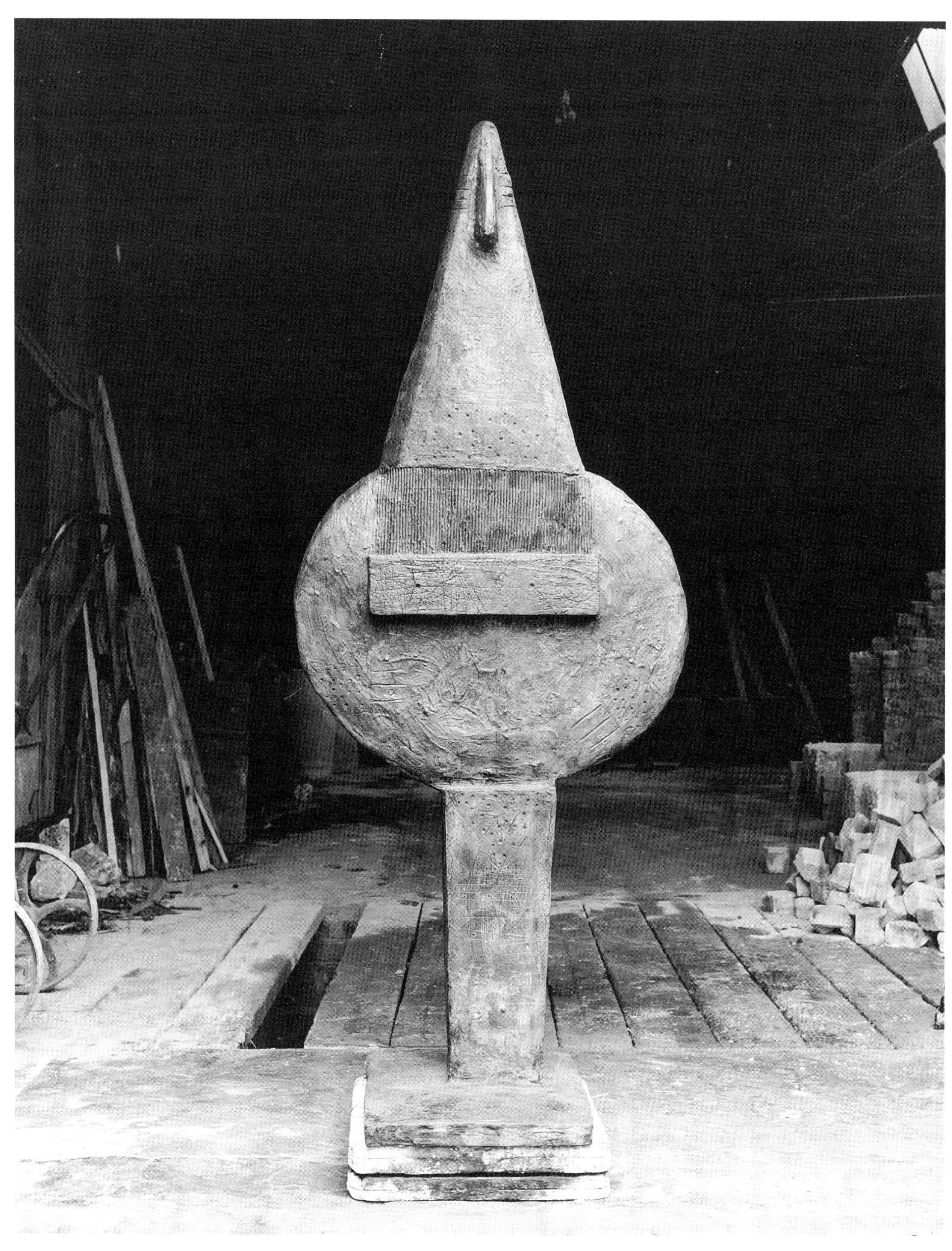

Idol 5 1957
bronze, 72 x 15¾ x 20 in/182.9 x 40 x 50.8 cm. Pisar collection, Paris

Bronze Idols and Untitled Paintings

DAVID SYLVESTER

There's an alluring word that has been widely abused in latter-day art writing: 'hieratic'. It is used to designate any frontal, symmetrical, compact, simplified, static image with a somewhat autocratic look. The word's true sense, consistent with its etymology, has to do with what is priestly – more broadly, with what pertains to sacred persons or functions. Of course hieratic art often is frontal, compact, simplified, *etc*, but not all the art that exhibits those qualities is hieratic. However, it's a word I would want to use in regard to some of Turnbull's sculptures.

Those sculptures are among the monolithic pieces which Turnbull made in plaster and cast in bronze between 1955 and 1958 and has made again since 1979 – motionless standing figures which have titles such as *Idol* and *Ancestral figure* and ovoid forms lying on their sides which have titles such as *Head* and *Metamorphosis*. There are also works such as *Aphrodite* in which an ovoid form is balanced across the top of a standing figure and which gave rise between 1958 and 1963 to stacked sculptures such as the *Oedipus* series.

These sculptures reflect an uninhibited commitment to the tradition in modernist sculpture which rejected the Renaissance imperative that classical Greek sculpture was to be the art's unique paragon and preferred to find models in various forms of archaic or primitive sculpture that seemed to evoke a human presence – or a divine presence – more directly than did sculpture that had been sidetracked into naturalism. The proper models were taken to be, for example, Palaeolithic carved ivory figurines, Neolithic figurines from Anatolia, carvings from Sumer, Egypt and the Cyclades, Archaic Greek sculpture such as the *Hera* from Samos, and then Romanesque carvings in both stone and wood and also masks and figures made by West African tribes such as the Dan, the Dogon and the Bambara. Those sorts of art were indeed for the most part hieratic. And it seems to me that there's a quality in some of Turnbull's figures which creates an expectation that, if some of them were placed in a simple well-lit building, it would become a temple.

Asked to justify an affirmation that there's something of the sacred in certain sculptures, one's immediate instinct is to say that either you see it or you don't. But if I do try and verbalize in the present instance, I would say that these sculptures derive this quality from their 'incredible lightness of being'. That lightness mainly belongs to the work of recent years. When Turnbull returned to making monolithic figures after an interval of about twenty years, the figures were much more slender in section than they had been before. What had once had the proportions of a column now had those of a plaque, a tablet. This was a demanding course to take, because a flimsy standing figure, even if it manages physically to stay erect, risks looking weak and pathetic. There's a well known Turnbull quote that reads: 'How little will suggest a head?' and in making his recent figures he seems to have been asking himself: How little substance can a structure have and still hold its own in space?

It seems pretty certain that those wafer-like sculptures of his owe a lot to the sort of paintings on which he embarked in 1957. He had previously made paintings that were the equivalent of his sculptures of heads. Now he started producing abstract monochromatic or duochromatic paintings as if asking the question: How little has to be done to a canvas to make it come alive? One of the recurrent answers was to put white paint all over the canvas with visible brushmarks (a usage in which Turnbull anticipated Robert Ryman).

But if the painting helped the sculpture I don't believe it did so to much effect for the first several years after the return to making idols. In those years the new degree of refinement, the increase in subtlety and suavity, were achieved at the not surprising expense of a loss of energy, a loss of pulse, in the images. The turning point came, I think, in 1986. The best of the sculptures since then have a wonderful poise in space, a vibrant balance matching what he had previously achieved in the *Aphrodite*, which recalls the perfect poise with which Indian women walk with vessels balanced on their heads.

The forms of these plaques owe something, Turnbull says, to the skateboards expertly used by his sons (here again the talk is essentially about poise). But I wonder whether these forms are not also an unconscious memory of the aircraft wings which he lived with for four years while a wartime pilot in the RAF. The plaques serenely carve their way through the air so that existence in space approaches a condition of pure movement or stance liberated from mass.

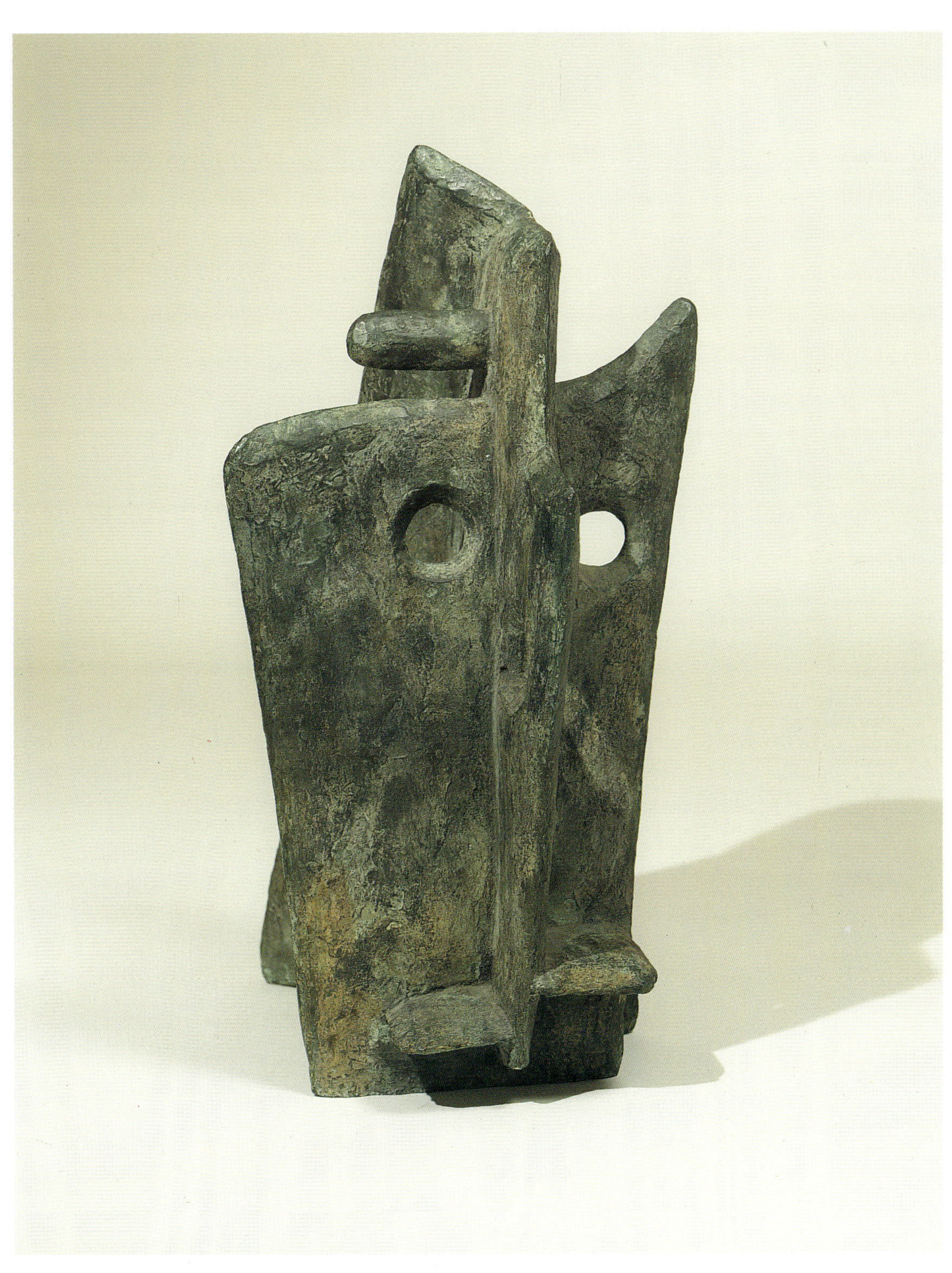

1 Horse 1946
bronze, 28 x 14 x 21 in/71.1 x 35.5 x 53.3 cm. The artist, courtesy Waddington Galleries

A Consistent Way of Thinking

PATRICK ELLIOTT

William Turnbull has been making sculpture and painting for exactly fifty years. He was born in Dundee in 1922. His father was an engineer in the shipyards, but during the Depression lost his job, obliging the young Turnbull to leave school at the age of fifteen to earn a living. His interest in art was fed largely through books. He had a multi-volume encyclopedia which covered everything from ancient art to modern art, via Egypt, India and Assyria; he also bought a number of the illustrated Phaidon art-books on the Impressionists and Post-Impressionists and received the latest colour comics from relatives in America. He did odd jobs as a labourer, including painting film-posters, but also attended art classes in Dundee two or three evenings a week. Turnbull was particularly fortunate with his teachers. His drawing teacher was the noted landscape-painter James McIntosh Patrick, and his instructor at illustration classes was Fred Mould, who worked for D.C. Thompson, the Dundee-based newspaper and magazine group. Observing Turnbull's talent for drawing, Mould invited him to work for D.C. Thompson in 1939. At the offices there were dozens of illustrators and cartoonists and it was this cosmopolitan group, many of whom had been to art school, who introduced Turnbull to the full breadth of modern art. He did, therefore, have a somewhat unorthodox, non-academic introduction to art, being in the position of an outsider, filtering images through books and magazines rather than through originals, and forgoing a full art-school education. In retrospect this non-hierarchical training, in which magazine illustrations, books on the Impressionists and Post-Impressionists, ethnographic art, evening-school instruction and casual conversation joined together in the same melting pot, proved the ideal education.

Turnbull was drafted into the Services in 1941, declared he wanted to be a pilot, and after a few rudimentary tests was passed fit for the RAF. Leaving Scotland for the first time he went to London for training and subsequently saw service in Canada, India and Ceylon. When the War was over he had the chance to become a full-time pilot but decided instead to continue with art. His colleagues at D.C. Thompson had spoken of the Slade School in London as the best art school in Britain, and so it was that he applied for a place there. Though he had scarcely drawn in nearly five years of service, he quickly got together a portfolio of work for

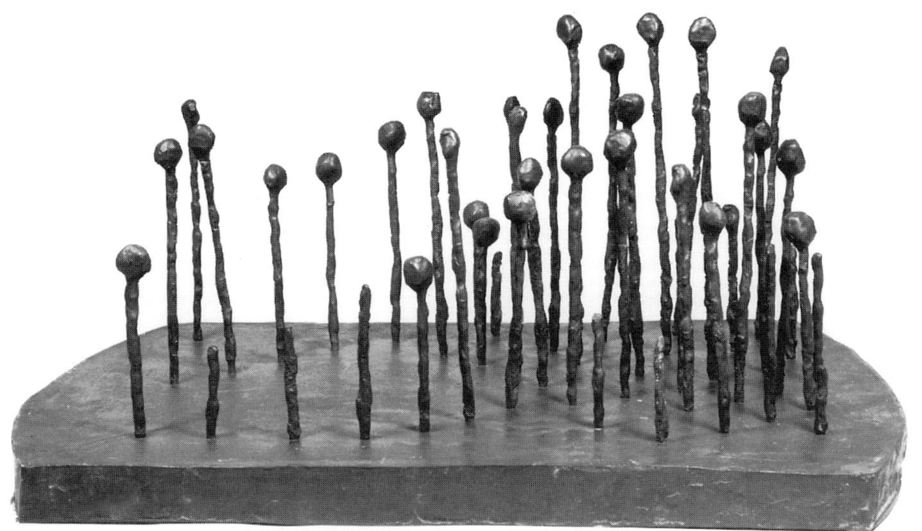

submission and was accepted into the painting department in the autumn of 1946. Just a week or two into the term he happened to wander into the sculpture department. He immediately felt at home in the workshop atmosphere and promptly transferred to the sculpture course. In the sculpture department he met a fellow Scot, Eduardo Paolozzi, who was in his third and final year at the Slade. The two struck up a close friendship. Both came from similar backgrounds and both felt as attracted to the modern imagery of magazine and comic-book illustrations as they were to the art of the Old Masters.

With most artists one can speak of juvenilia and student work developing, in later years, into something more mature and fully formed, but Turnbull by-passed the usual development curve and began with work of real authority. One of his very first sculptures, *Horse* (plate 1), made at the Slade in 1946, is remarkably prophetic of work the artist would make forty years later. At the time Paolozzi was making sculptures in cement – a very unusual method which contrasted with the traditional approach of modelling in clay favoured at the Slade – and Turnbull adopted a similarly direct method, modelling with wet plaster on a metal armature. The *Horse* was made by this method; originally it bore fine, engraved marks over the surface and was painted yellow. On the one hand this work owes something to Cubism with its

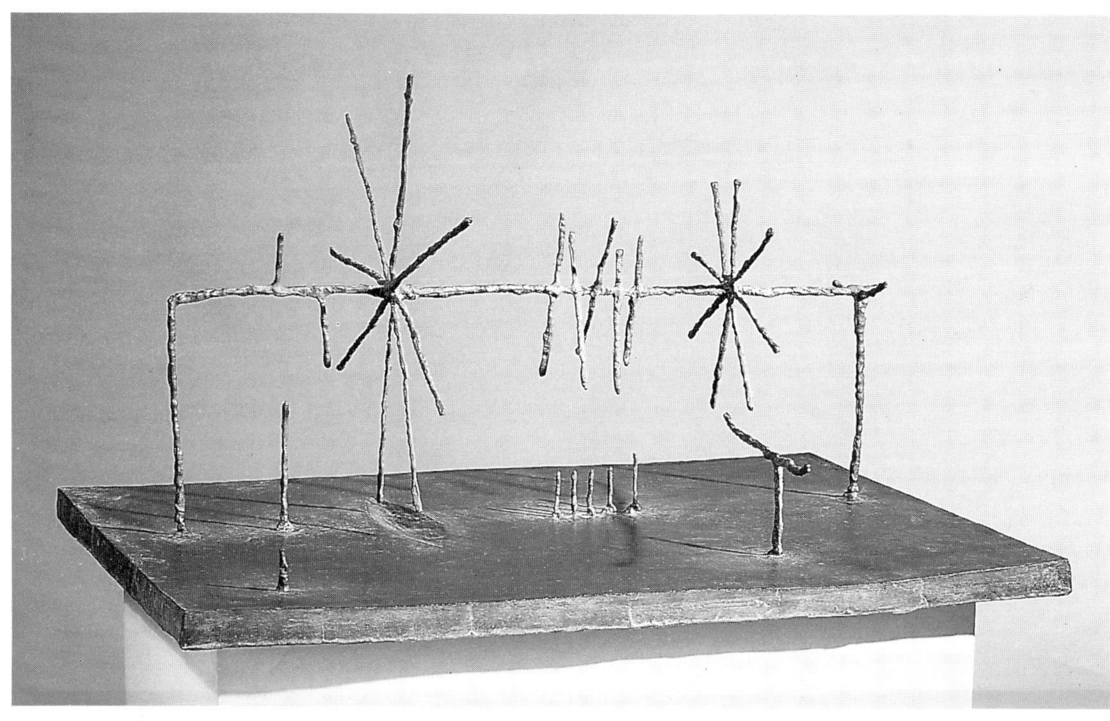

interlocking flat planes that could almost be disassembled, and on the other it shows the clarity and lucidity of form that would characterize Turnbull's entire œuvre. Other works of the period include a *Mask* of 1946, made in cement with string stuck on to the surface, several pieces made from copper sheets and rods soldered together (a technique he learned from an uncle in Dundee who was a coppersmith) and a number of planar constructions made of soldered metal rods.

In 1947 Turnbull spent six weeks travelling in Italy. It was with a certain feeling of guilt that he felt unmoved by many of the masters of the High Renaissance and unable to subscribe to the notion, still popular at that time, that art had developed on an upward curve. He liked the work of Giotto and Piero della Francesca, but he also felt himself drawn to Greek *kouros* figures and Egyptian art and to the pots and oddments one finds in ethnographic museums. It remains the case that Turnbull's art is closer in spirit to the ancient, non-classical arts found in the British Museum than to the naturalism of the Old Masters on display at the National Gallery. On the way back to London he visited Paris for a few days, staying with Paolozzi who

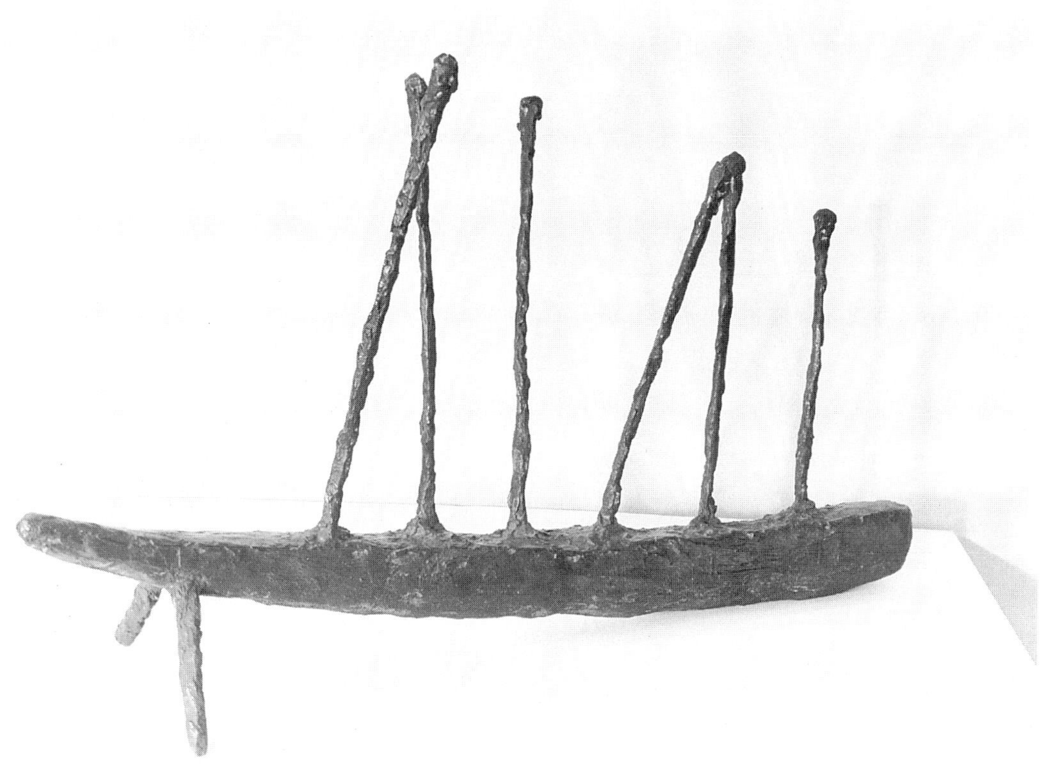

had moved there the previous year.

In the public consciousness, the major art movement in London in the immediate post-War years was Neo-Romanticism, which owed much to the art of William Blake and to the 'visionary' landscapes of Samuel Palmer. It was a movement fostered by Graham Sutherland and John Piper and taken up by a number of artists of Turnbull's generation including John Minton and John Craxton. Turnbull, who felt completely alien to the English Romantic tradition, was more attracted to Paris and moved there in 1948, managing to have his grant transferred. To satisfy the conditions of the grant he signed on for a course at the Grande Chaumière art school in Montparnasse but never attended the lessons. He found himself a cheap room in a hotel on the Ile St Louis, in the heart of the city, and later rented a *chambre de bonne* in Montmartre. Unknown to his landlady, Turnbull would smuggle bags of plaster upstairs to his little room and began to people it with extraordinary, stick-like sculptures.

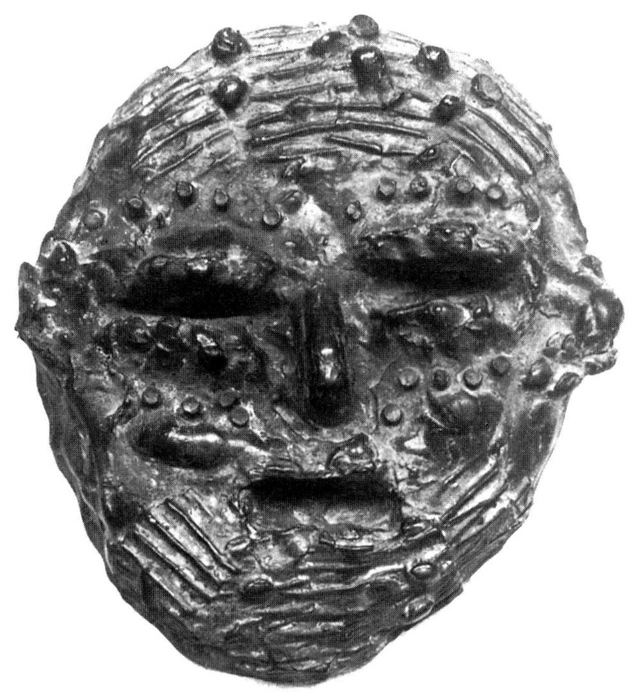

In the late 1940s Paris was still very much the capital of the art world, providing home to a remarkable variety of artists and writers from all over the globe. Everyone met at the cafés, allowing newcomers to engage in Parisian social life and meet fellow artists. A number of young British artists settled in Paris after the War, including Paolozzi (of whom Turnbull saw a great deal), William Gear, Raymond Mason and William Chattaway. Others, such as Lucian Freud, spent regular, extended visits in Paris. At that time meeting artists, even the most famous, was straightforward: one got an introduction, met them at a bar or knocked at their door. It was thus that Turnbull met Léger, Giacometti, Brancusi, Hélion and others. Giacometti proved a particularly strong influence. The Swiss sculptor, who had associated with the Surrealists before the War, had only recently begun making a series of tall, attenuated figures and another of lone, striding men. Turnbull and Nigel Henderson, a friend from the Slade, went to see Giacometti at his tiny studio in Montparnasse, and Turnbull met him again on many occasions thereafter. During 1949 Turnbull made a series of works which relate to some of Giacometti's pre-War Surrealist compositions as well as to the *City Square* of 1948 in which small stick-figures walk across a rectangular base, apparently oblivious of one another. Using

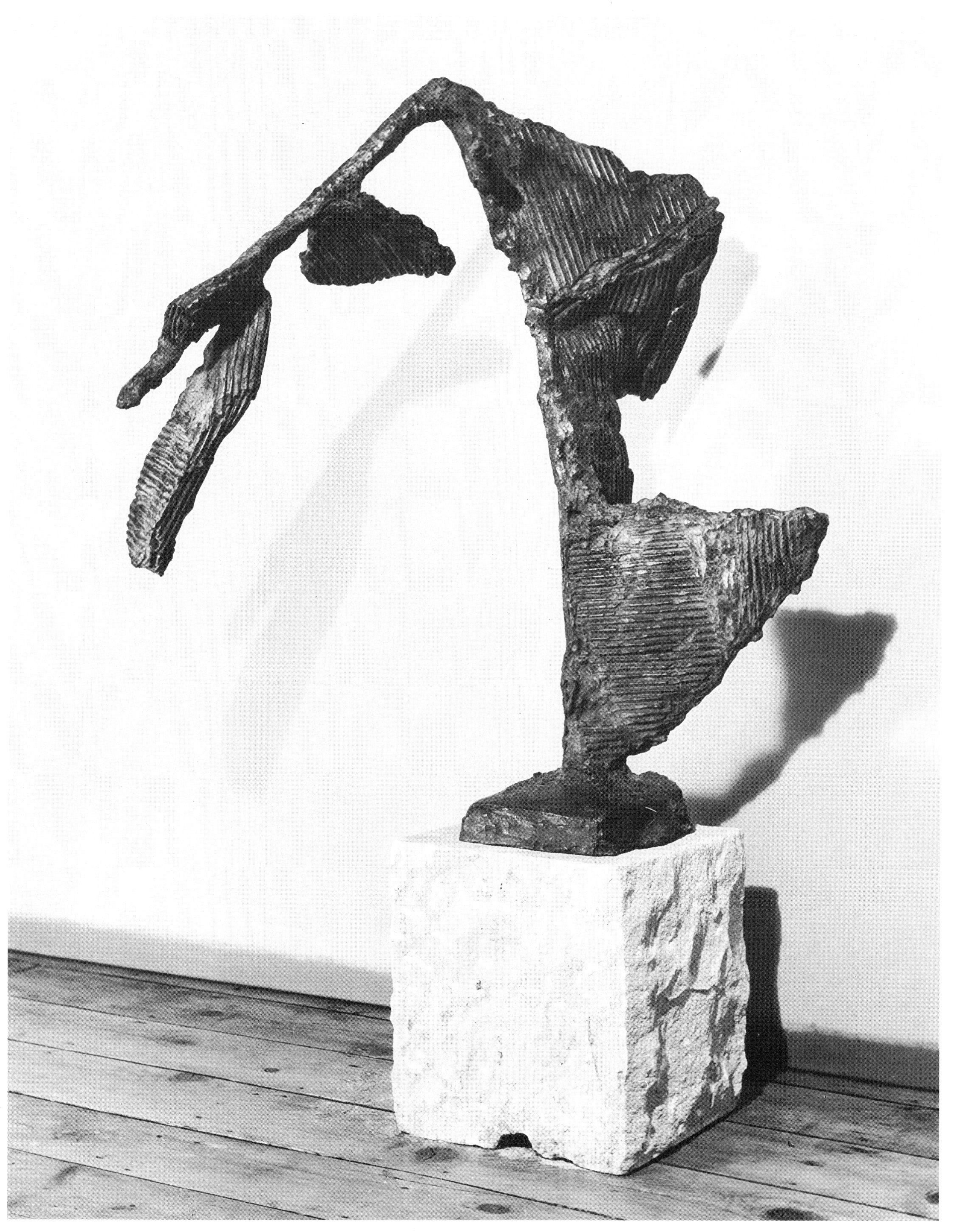

6 Pegasus 1954
bronze, 35 x 17½ x 29¼ in/88.9 x 19.1 x 74.3 cm. Private collection, London

a similar base device, Turnbull made several very linear works, modelled in plaster on a thin wire armature (and later cast in bronze), such as *Mobile Stabile* (plate 3), *Forms on a base* and *Game* (plate 2), in which the stunted rods can be plucked from their sockets and placed in alternative arrangements. Turnbull was a keen billiards and pinball player at this time, and some of these works, for example the wooden *Playground*, call to mind the bases of such ball-games with their various channels, holes and obstacles. Another of Turnbull's interests was fish, particularly the way they hang motionless in the water and then suddenly shift direction together. He made a number of visits to an aquarium in Paris and produced two large mobile sculptures based on the movement of fish, including *Hanging sculpture* of 1949.

Apart from the base-works and the mobiles, Turnbull made several free-standing, three-dimensional pieces. *Heavy insect* (plate 4) is a memorably curious sculpture (the quality of the absurd in Turnbull's work is too often ignored). It sprang from an experience we all share of lying on the ground on a hot day and seeing insects very close up, crawling about in the grass. It is an insect as other insects might see it: big, odd, a bit like a dinosaur. The largest of these works is *Horse* (plate 7), which is like a three-dimensional diagram of the structure of the animal, only here there seem to be too many limbs. Turnbull's love of Kafka's writings informed sculptures such as these: Gregor Samsa, the man-insect 'hero' of *Metamorphosis*, would be at home in this world.

In February 1950 Turnbull and Paolozzi had a joint exhibition, organized by their friend David Sylvester (who had been semi-resident in Paris for two years) at the Hanover Gallery in London. The gallery, run by Erica Brausen, was among the most dynamic in London at that time, showing work by Giacometti, Freud and Bacon in the early 1950s. Turnbull exhibited a dozen works, most of them in plaster. Shortly after his return to Paris Turnbull was selected for an exhibition of work by young artists at the Galerie Maeght (Maeght later became Giacometti's dealer). He remained in Paris until October but his grant from the Slade had run out and without a permit to work in France a job in England seemed more likely. Thus he settled in London at the end of 1950 and the following year found a flat in Hampstead and a job teaching experimental design at the Central School of Art. William Johnstone, a Scot who had produced some unusual abstract paintings between the Wars, had taken over as principal of the school in 1947 and began to employ some of the most radical young artists working in London, fostering a course styled upon that at the Bauhaus. Among the new teachers were

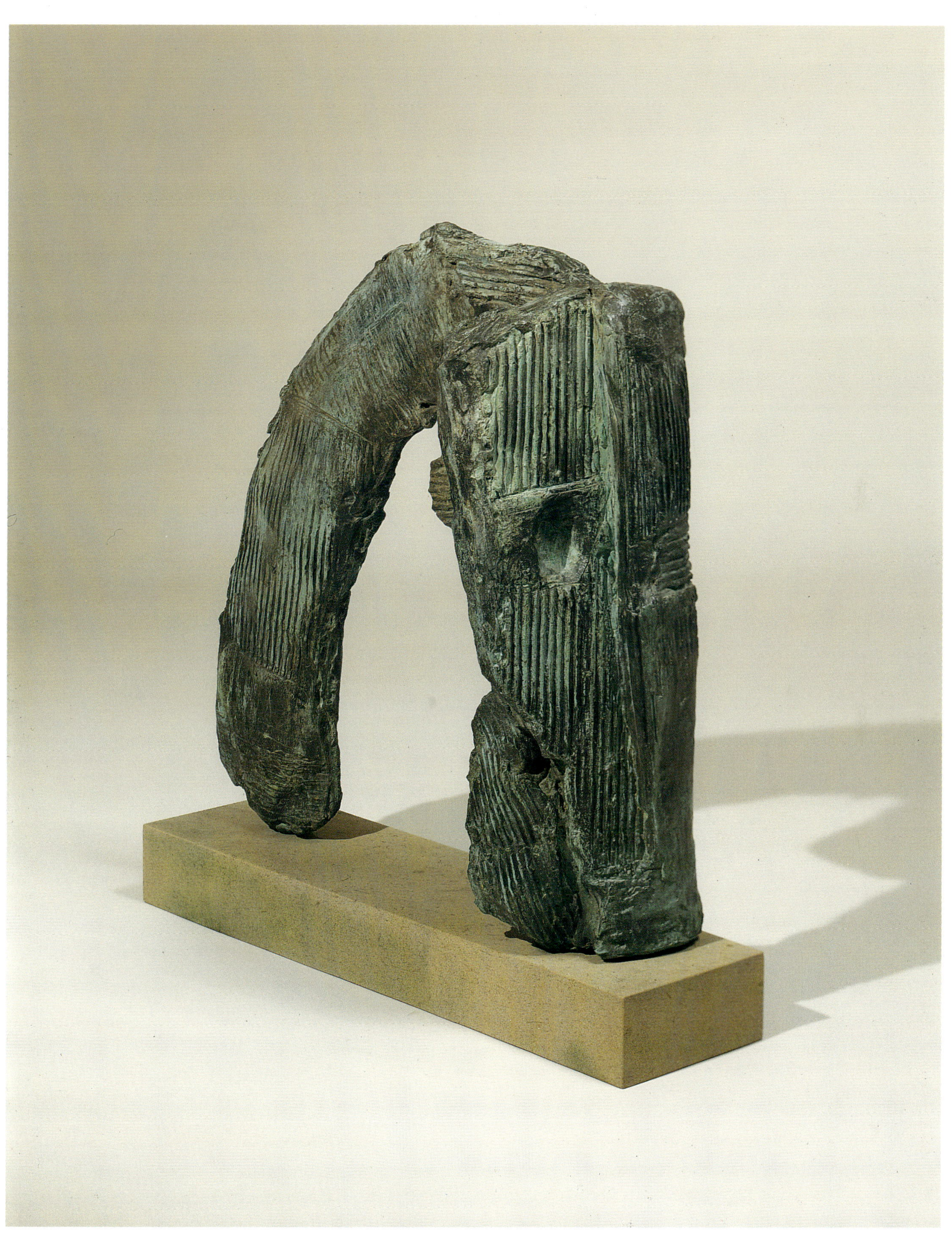

7 Horse 1954, bronze on stone base, bronze 26⅜ x 27 x 9 in/
67 x 68.6 x 24.1 cm, base 3¼ x 29 x 7¼ in/8.3 x 73.6 x 18.4 cm. Edition of 2. Private collection, London

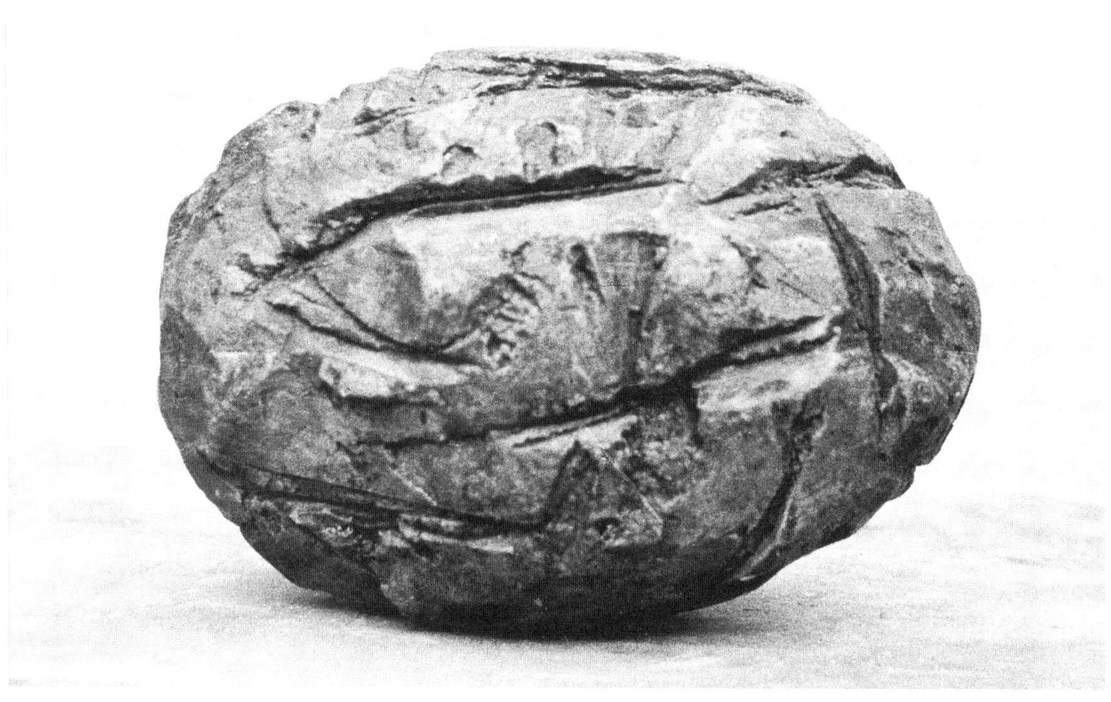

Paolozzi, Patrick Heron, Nigel Henderson and Alan Davie, who each taught a non-curricular course one day a week, allowing them to continue for the rest of the week on their own work.

In 1952, Turnbull, who had only recently turned thirty, had a solo exhibition at the Hanover Gallery and was included in an exhibition in the British pavilion at the Venice Biennale. This show, *New Aspects of British Sculpture*, had been selected by Herbert Read and included sculptures by Robert Adams, Kenneth Armitage, Lynn Chadwick, Reg Butler, Geoffrey Clarke, Bernard Meadows and Paolozzi; Henry Moore's work was shown outside the building. Some of these sculptors depicted the human figure in an angular, contorted form, and in his catalogue introduction Read wrote that their work symbolized a 'geometry of fear' – a term that has since become synonymous with British sculpture of the period. The term was not much welcomed by the artists though, for their aims and methods were more divergent and wide-ranging than some commentators indicated. Turnbull, for one, had not even met several members of this group he was said to belong to, and his work demonstrates a balance, clarity and simplicity that has little to do with the *Angst*-ridden concerns prevalent in much post-War art.

Turnbull was included in another exhibition early that year, *Young Sculptors*, shown at the Institute of Contemporary Arts. Created by a group including Herbert Read, Roland Penrose, Peter Watson, Robert Melville and E.C. Gregory, the ICA was launched in the years immediately after the war and moved into a permanent address in Dover Street in 1950: there it became the focal point for radical new art in London. Artists would drop in for a drink and a meal at the bar and a chat with fellow members. Turnbull went there regularly almost as soon as he returned to London, and for him it filled the place the Left Bank cafés had occupied in his life in Paris. Other visitors included Richard Hamilton, Paolozzi and Henderson, and writers such as Lawrence Alloway, Michael Compton and Reyner Banham. Turnbull was among this younger element which in 1952 formed a splinter group within the ICA, the Independent Group. Their regular, formal discussions ranged from contemporary art to cybernetics, science fiction, technology and magazine illustrations, and these interests were reflected in their art and in the exhibitions they organized at the ICA. Without being set up as a 'counter-movement', the Independent Group challenged the dominion that the landscape-oriented, St Ives and Neo-Romantic aesthetics held over British art. One theme which recurred again and again in their meetings was the idea that art had not developed in a linear, progressive way, and that 5000-year-old pots, African sculptures and Western films could seem far more relevant to contemporary concerns than many modern paintings. Art was a mosaic of all kinds of images, a repository which knew no borders. It had a parallel in post-War magazines which might feature photographs of tribesmen next to photographs of the moon, strip-cartoons next to political commentary, adverts for cleaning products next to reproductions of highbrow paintings: they were all there on an equal footing. This conception of art, which Turnbull had innocently formulated in his youth, would be one of the principal driving forces in his work.

Turnbull's sculpture of this period was much concerned with line: most of the works were skeletal structures made from plaster on a metal armature. Some suggested movement while others such as *Game* and the hanging mobiles actually incorporated movement. He even made a weathervane, painted bright red, for Roland Penrose in about 1952. The hanging works relate to the mobiles of Alexander Calder but more crucially to the art and writings of Paul Klee.

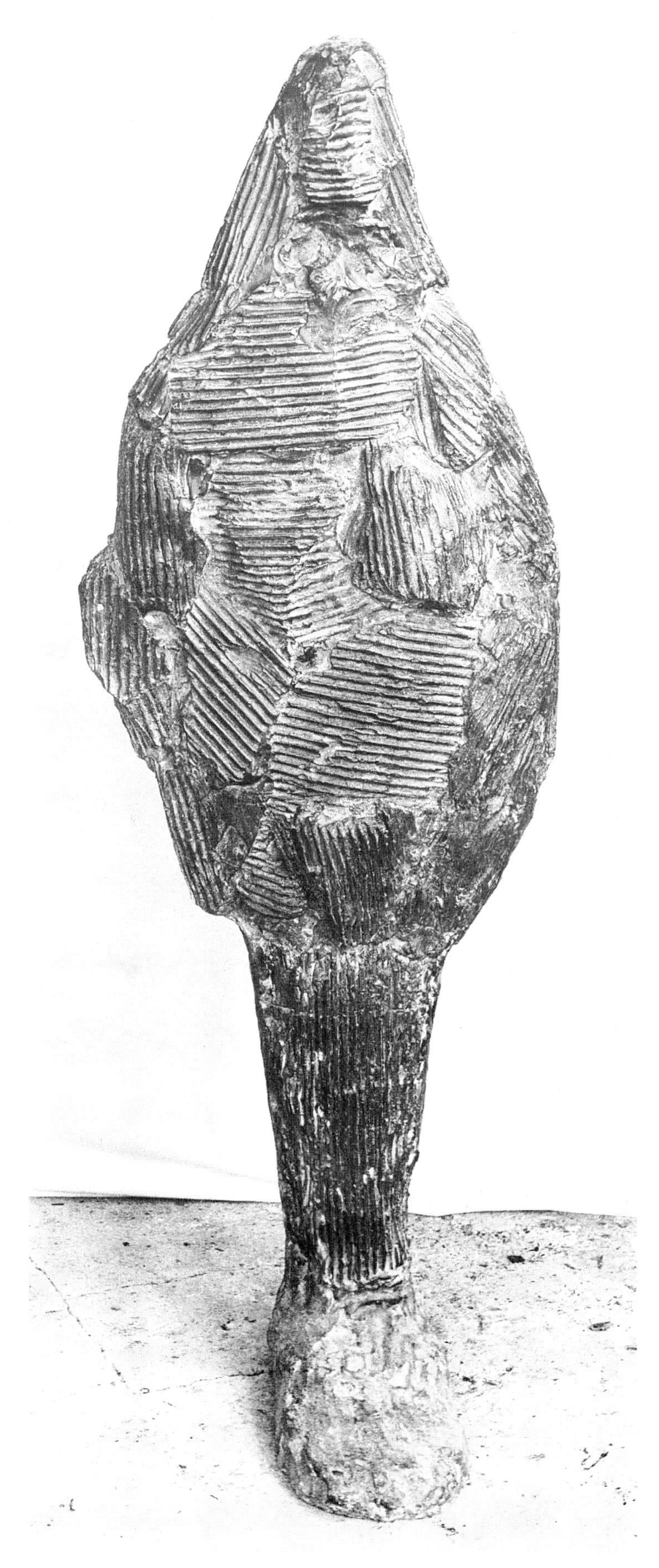

9 Female figure 1955
bronze, 47¾ x 16½ x 13¾ in/121.3 x 41.9 x 34.9 cm. Edition of 4. Private collection, London

Even before going to Paris Turnbull had been interested in Klee's art and writings, and had seen a major show of Klee's work held in London in 1946. If Klee had taken walks with a line, Turnbull took walks with plaster-covered pieces of wire.

In 1953 he moved away from the thin, linear structures to solid, three-dimensional forms in a series of small *Masks*, each slightly less than a foot in diameter (plate 5). In making the *Masks*, Turnbull constructed a circular bed of clay into which he pressed objects and made marks in an almost random way, though the imprints always carried just enough information to suggest the human head. He then made plaster casts of the clays, to give a negative impression of what he had made, each of the marks made into the clay translating as a projection in the plaster (and subsequent bronze casts). In this series Turnbull was not so much interested in creating a facial expression as in treating surface as a kind of skin – rather as a mask is a

▷

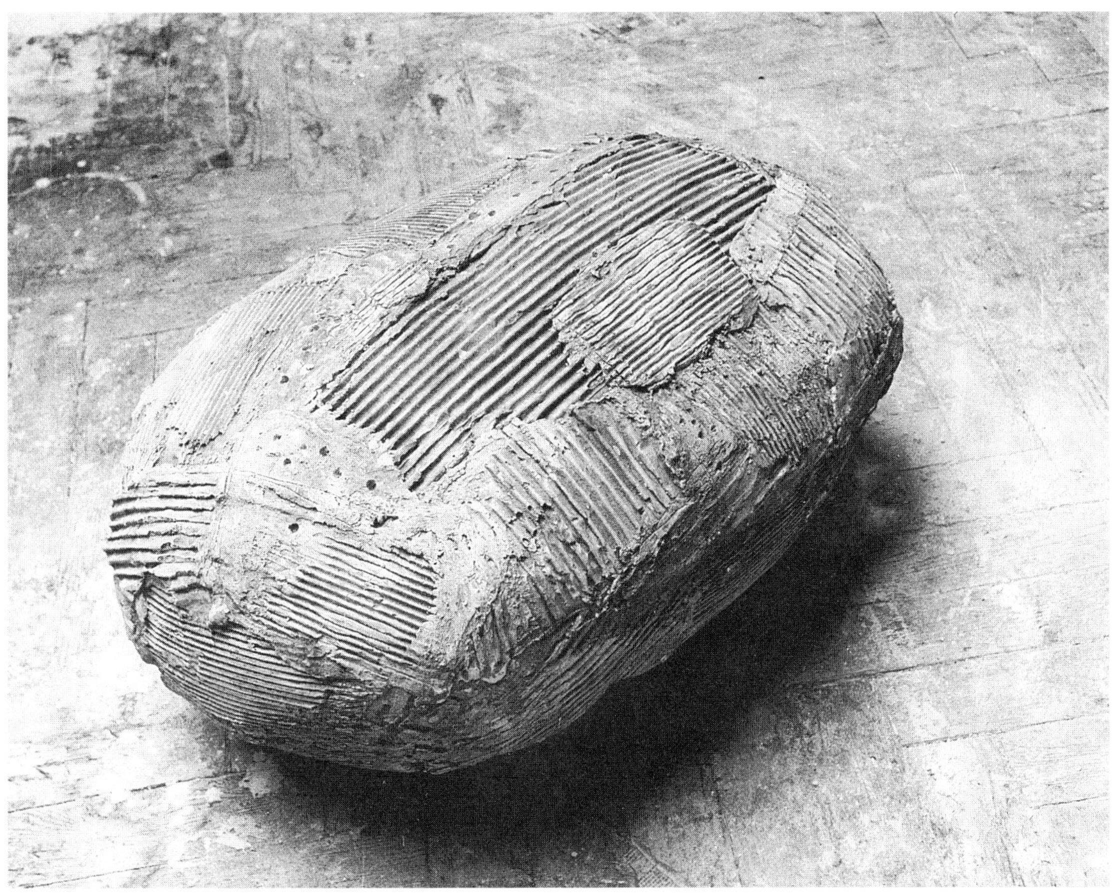

10
Metamorphosis
1955
bronze
13½ x 18¼ x 25¾ in/
34.3 x 46.4 x
65.4 cm
The artist, courtesy
Waddington Galleries

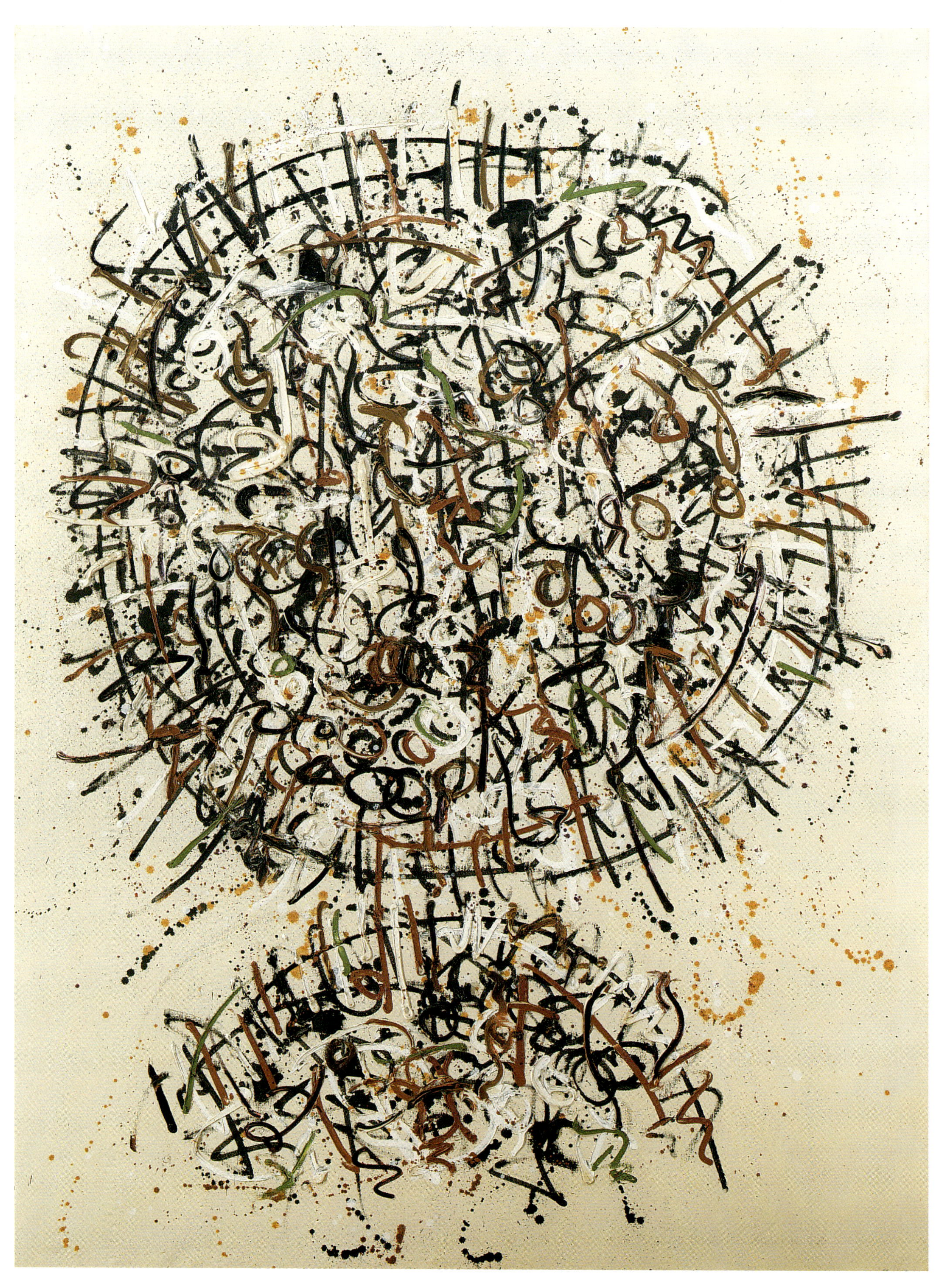

11 Head (calligraphic) 1956
oil on canvas, 60 x 44 in/152.4 x 111.8 cm. Private collection, London

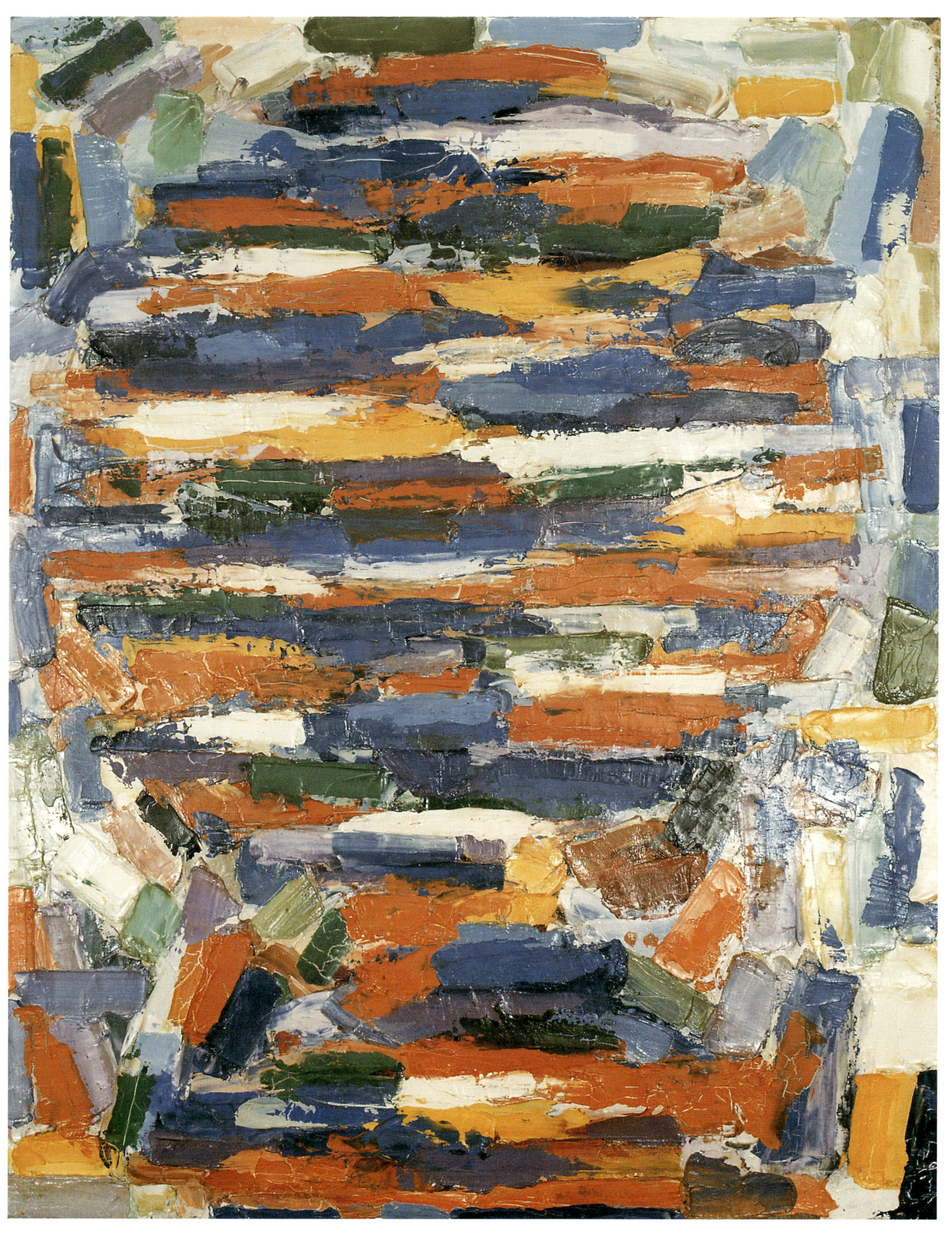

12 Mask 1955–56
oil on canvas, 40 x 34 in/101.6 x 86.4 cm. Swindon Museum and Art Gallery

skin – over which the eye travels. In looking at the *Masks* one is aware, above all, of their surface: each is like a miniature landscape. Some parts are busy while others are smooth and others evenly ridged, and these qualities affect the way the eyes scan each work. Turnbull had observed similar effects in Chinese Shang bronzes and also in the Benin bronzes at the British Museum, where one is more aware of the skin or surface than of the three-dimensional mass of the work.

Pegasus of 1954 (plate 6) was begun in the same way Turnbull had made the linear works of the late 1940s and early 1950s, being constructed on a branch-like metal armature. Here, though, he filled in the spaces between some of the right-angled rods, and gave them a corrugated surface texture. It is like the 1950 *Horse* with wings, hence the title. The 1954 *Horse* (plate 7) is the first of the fully three-dimensional, non-linear works.

The final appearance of each *Mask* had much to do with chance, for the marks only became legible once each work had been reversed through the casting process. Chance and chaos, subjected to the artist's control, have played a crucial role in Turnbull's work. He never makes preliminary drawings and rarely makes maquettes for his paintings or sculptures, preferring

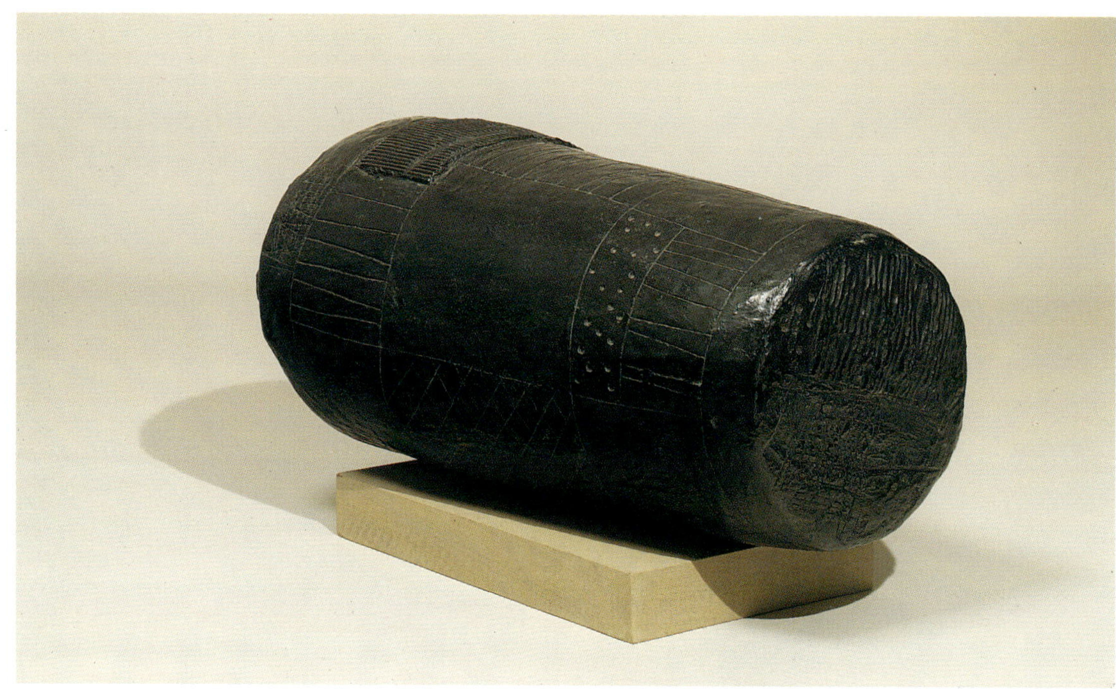

13
Drum 1956
bronze on stone base,
bronze 15 x 29½ x
15 in/38.1 x 74.9 x
38.1 cm, base 2¾ x
20 x 12⅝ in/
7 x 50.8 x 32 cm
The artist, courtesy
Waddington Galleries

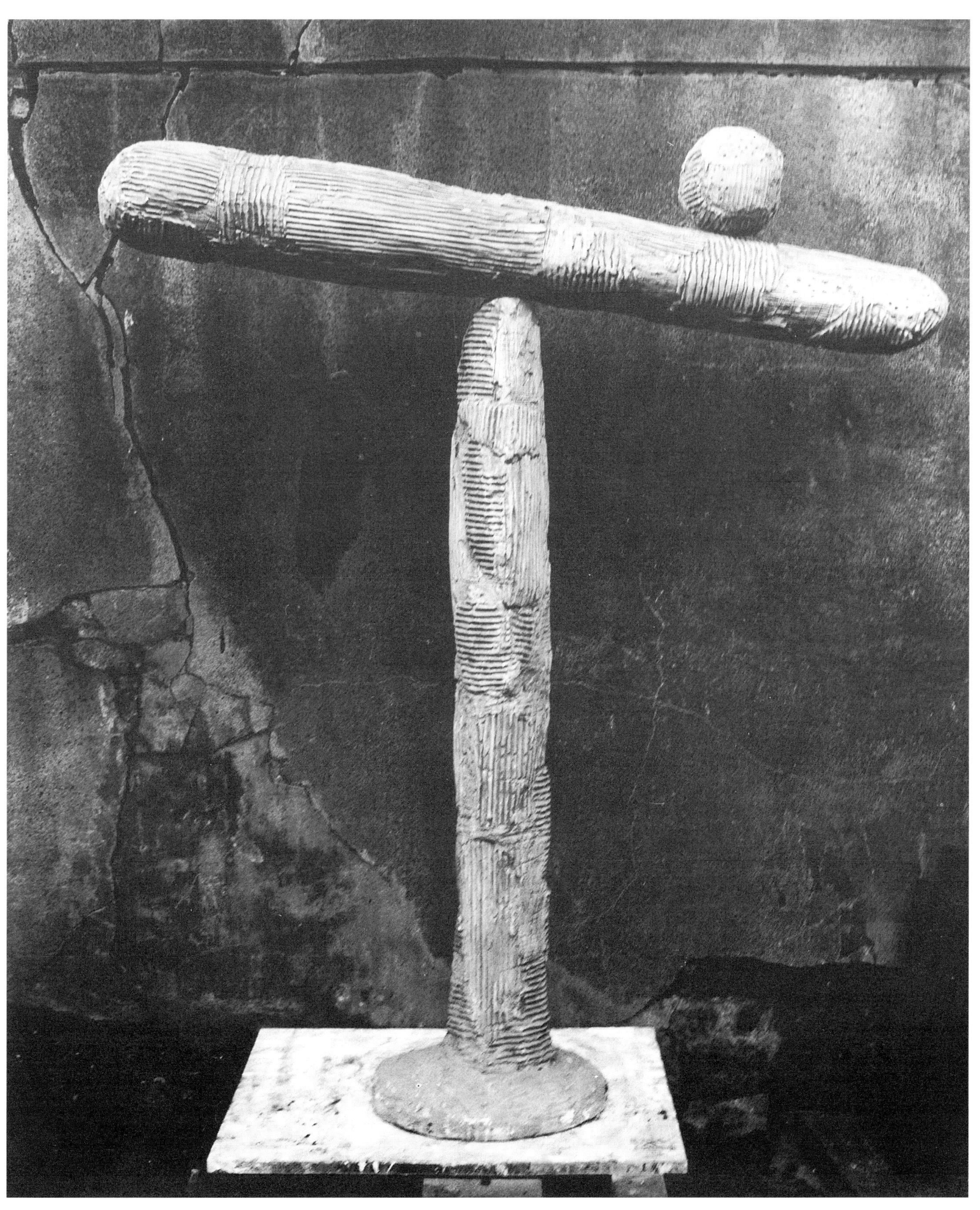

14 Permutation Sculpture 1956
bronze, 58 x 10½ x 49 in/147.3 x 26.7 x 124.5 cm. Ossorio collection, New York

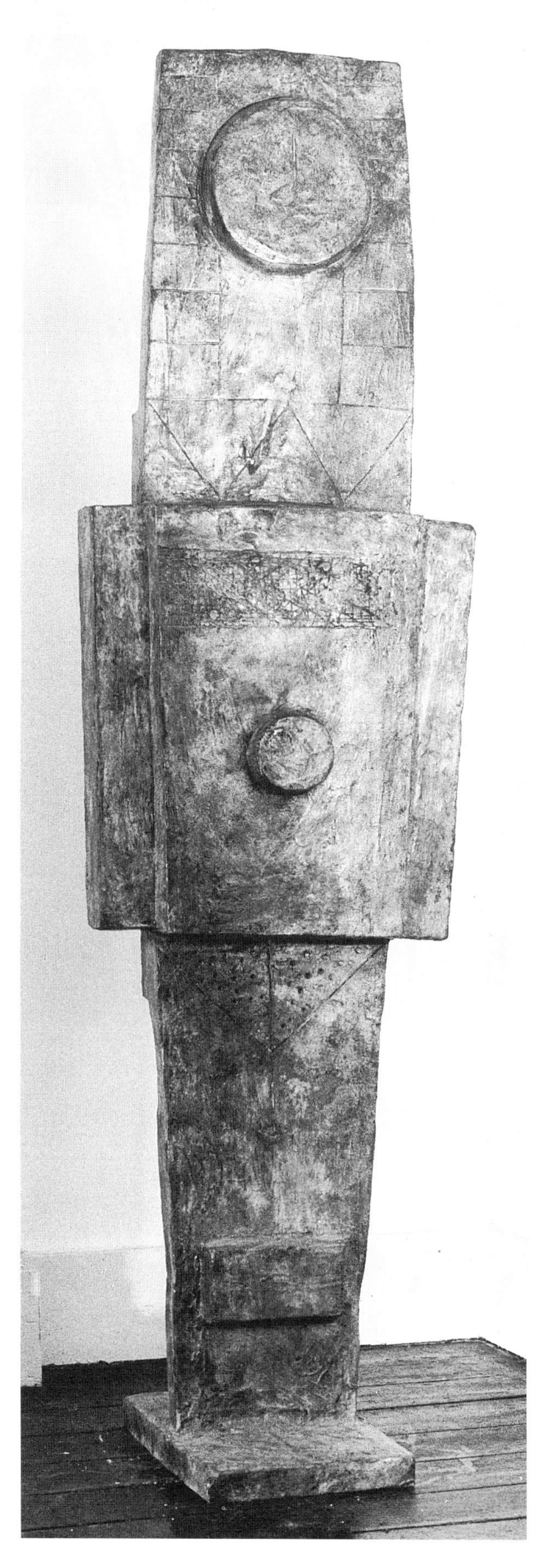

15 Totemic figure 1957
bronze, 61¼ x 16¾ x 14½ in/153 x 42.5 x 36.8 cm. Edition of 4. Private collection, London

to develop the work in its full scale. His interest in chance came from a number of sources –
in part from Surrealism but above all from Paul Klee, who stressed the idea of the artist as a
natural, creative being from whom forms should spring in a natural, non-formulaic way.
Turnbull's art has also been greatly enriched by his voracious reading, his interests ranging
from the Existentialist writings of Camus and Sartre, which he consumed in Paris, to popular
science fiction. In the early 1950s he became interested in oriental philosophies, and was particularly impressed by the ideas which informed Zen painting. The Zen artist projected his idea
in an instant with the flick of the brush, without rationalizing about such matters as composition. This ideal was somewhat harder to achieve in three-dimensional sculpture, but by
making stabbing marks into the clay, as he did in making the *Masks*, Turnbull neatly circum-
vented the deliberative, often highly technical procedures that are peculiar to sculpture.

He developed this process in a series of *Heads* made in the mid-1950s (*e.g.* plate 8). These
sculptures, all scarred and lacerated, or bearing the imprint of corrugated paper, are like
Brancusi's perfectly polished *Muse* reinterpreted for the nuclear age: their resemblance to hand-
grenades and bombs is probably not accidental. Whereas Brancusi's heads have the appearance of newly laid eggs, Turnbull's, though calm and compact, look as if they had been to
hell and back, their features so battered that one scarcely notices them. As with the *Masks*, these
Heads can be read as miniature landscapes, covered with valleys, crevices and hills. In their
emphasis on surface they are, paradoxically, like relief sculptures in the round. They do not
even have a correct way up and, fitting nicely into the hands, are meant to be fingered and
turned about. The surfaces of two of the *Heads* (*Drumhead*, 1955, and *Head* 2, 1955 [plate 8])
were created by sticking corrugated paper on to the wet plaster (most of his works from this
date were made directly in plaster rather than clay) and then pulling it off to leave an imprint
of gnarled but rhythmic grooves. The chance element involved in doing this was quite different
from that proposed by some of the Surrealists who, in theory if not always in practice, sought
an entirely automatic art form; and it was different also to the approach of many of his con-
temporaries – Paolozzi for example – who favoured collage, for with collage the artist makes
very deliberate selections regarding the image or form that will be cut out and incorporated
into the work.

Turnbull is most widely known for his sculpture, but throughout his career he has made
paintings. Generally he works in one medium for some months and then in the other. The two

▷

16 29–1958
oil on canvas, 60 x 60 in/152.4 x 152.4 cm. The artist, courtesy Waddington Galleries

17 Painting (black) 1957
oil on canvas, 78 x 69 in/198.1 x 175.3cm. Private collection, courtesy Raymond Danowski

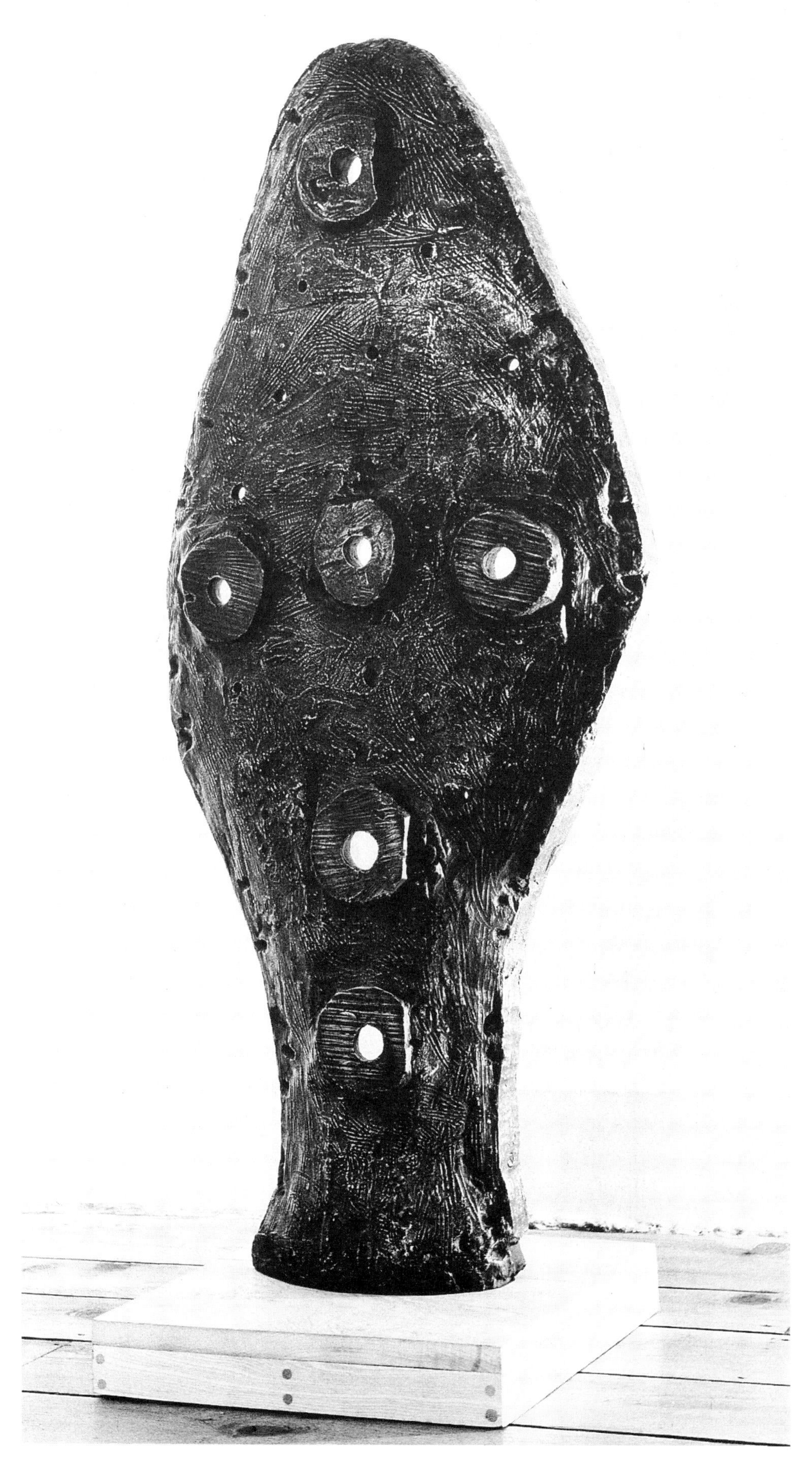

18 Source 1958
bronze, 49½ x 21½ x 3½ in/125.7 x 54.6 x 8.9 cm. Edition of 4. Private collection, London

arts are very separate practices for him. The paintings are not of or about the sculptures and *vice versa*, rather the paintings deal with the language and process of painting and the sculpture with the language and process of sculpture. Nevertheless, strong parallels exist between his work in both media. The paintings, brush drawings and prints of these years, until 1956, used the head as their motif, reducing it to its most basic form, a circle mounted on a vertical stalk. Just as the element of chance was crucial to the sculptures, so it was to the paintings. He adopted a number of techniques deliberately designed to limit his control over the development of each work: the control element came in deciding when to stop and when to continue. Sometimes he painted with short, almost random marks which coalesced into a head shape (*Mask*, 1955–56[plate 12]). At other times he would paint in a calligraphic manner, moving the loaded brush so quickly that he could not determine the exact character of each mark; or would splatter skeins of paint on to the paper or canvas from which a primitive head-form, not unlike those made by Dubuffet, would emerge (*Head (calligraphic)*, 1956 [plate 11]). Regarding his favoured motif, Turnbull commented that: "The word 'Head' meant for me what I imagined the word 'Landscape' had meant for some painters – a format that could carry different loadings. Almost anything could be a head – and a head almost anything – given the slightest clue to the decoding … I wanted to make a head-object as autonomous as a football."[1]

In 1955 he made the first of a long series, still in progress, of totemic, standing figures. As with some of the *Masks* and *Heads*, the surfaces of several of the earliest of these figures were made by pressing corrugated paper into the soft plaster (*Female figure*, 1955 [plate 9]), and Turnbull would also scratch and press marks into the surface. He did not set out with a particular, resolved form in mind, rather the process of making the work led him to improvise. Most of these figures are a foot or two smaller than life-size and are designed to stand directly on the floor, not on a plinth. It has been a feature of Turnbull's sculpture that he works in a format slightly over or under life-size, as if to emphasize that the works are not figures in a literal sense. The series of five standing figures entitled *Idol* have a clear parentage in the primitive idols found in ethnographic museums – such museums have been a vital source of inspiration for Turnbull – but the title is also a pun on the screen idols of Hollywood. *War goddess*, a busty, broad-hipped figure, can thus be seen as a composite creature, uniting the primitive fertility goddess with the screen goddess, be it Marilyn Monroe or Jayne Mansfield. Although Turnbull's work relates less obviously to the culture of popular imagery than does

1. 'Head Semantics' in *Uppercase 4*, 1960.

the art of Richard Hamilton, Peter Blake, Paolozzi or Warhol, to name a few, it embraces the same concerns but in a different way. Another work, *Screwhead* of 1958, calls to mind Brancusi's severely monolithic *Kiss* sculptures, but its immediate sources were a chocolate vending-machine Turnbull had seen at an underground station, and a grandfather clock. The face of the clock has metamorphosed into a head and the pull-out trays of the machine have been transformed into breasts. Turnbull's work is full of these unexpected, usually hidden references to old and new forms, high art and low art, Western and non-Western. The constancy of certain elemental forms in different cultures throughout the ages is one of the mainsprings of his art, and it is partly this multivalency of meaning and source that gives his art its formal and metaphorical richness.

The *Idol* and *Standing figures* of the second half of the 1950s are unambiguously frontal, in the way that Archaic Greek art and ancient Egyptian art is. Classical and Renaissance sculpture, indeed Henry Moore's sculpture, is concerned with the rotating viewpoint, so that the viewer is inclined to walk around the work and discover a series of changing compositions. Turnbull, like Giacometti, was more concerned with establishing an arresting, frontal image (as Giacometti once said, you don't walk around a person you meet, so why do it in sculpture?), one which tends to dominate space and radiate out into it. In an article published in 1968 Turnbull remarked that "The work must be perceived instantly, not read in time",[2] and he has always remained consistent to that ideal, avoiding all suggestion of narrative. His figures do not wash their feet, as Degas's do, play the guitar, as Lipchitz's do, or walk or point, as Giacometti's sometimes do. Instead they are faceless, ageless and totemic. This is not to say that one should not walk around his sculptures, but to acknowledge that most have a definite front, sides and back. The backs are often unexpectedly different from the fronts.

Sungazer and *Permutation sculpture* (plate 14), both of 1956, were the first in a series in which a horizontal beam was balanced on a vertical, standing form. In the case of *Sungazer* that 'beam' was the most elongated of the heads made the previous year, while in *Permutation sculpture* the various elements were partly interchangeable. The vertical forms of these sculptures are close to the Archaic Greek figures and architectural columns which Turnbull admired, and the corrugated surface even echoed the fluted drapery of some of these works. The balance in sculptures such as these suggests something of the male and female, the *yin* and *yang* in equilibrium. *Sungazer* featured in the celebrated exhibition *This is Tomorrow*, held at the Whitechapel Art

2. 'Notes on Sculpture' in *Studio International*, November 1968.

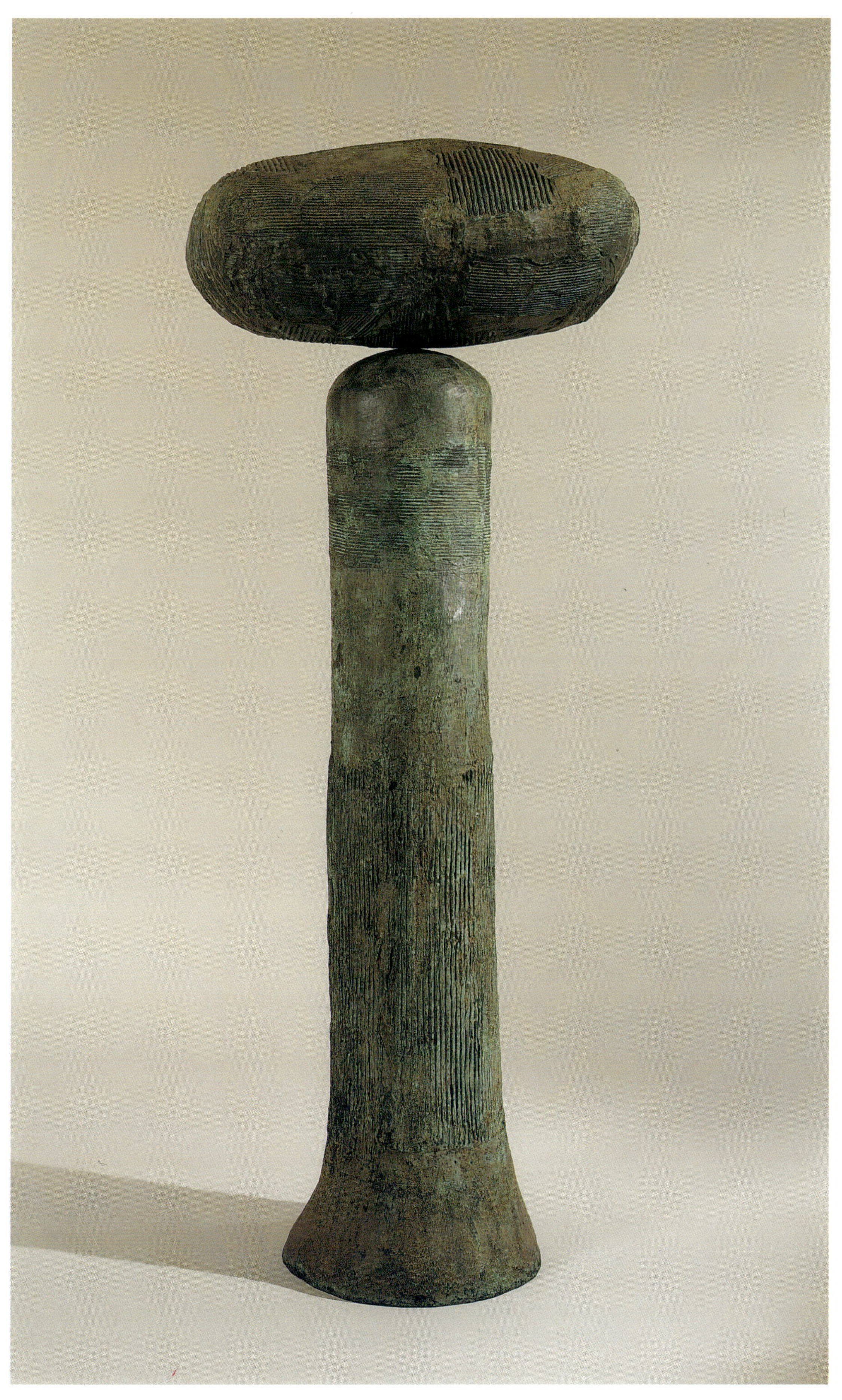

19 Aphrodite 1958
bronze, 74 x 29 x 19½ in/188 x 73.7 x 49.5 cm. The artist, courtesy Waddington Galleries

20   28-1958

oil on canvas, 70 x 70 in/177.8 x 177.8cm. The artist, courtesy Waddington Galleries

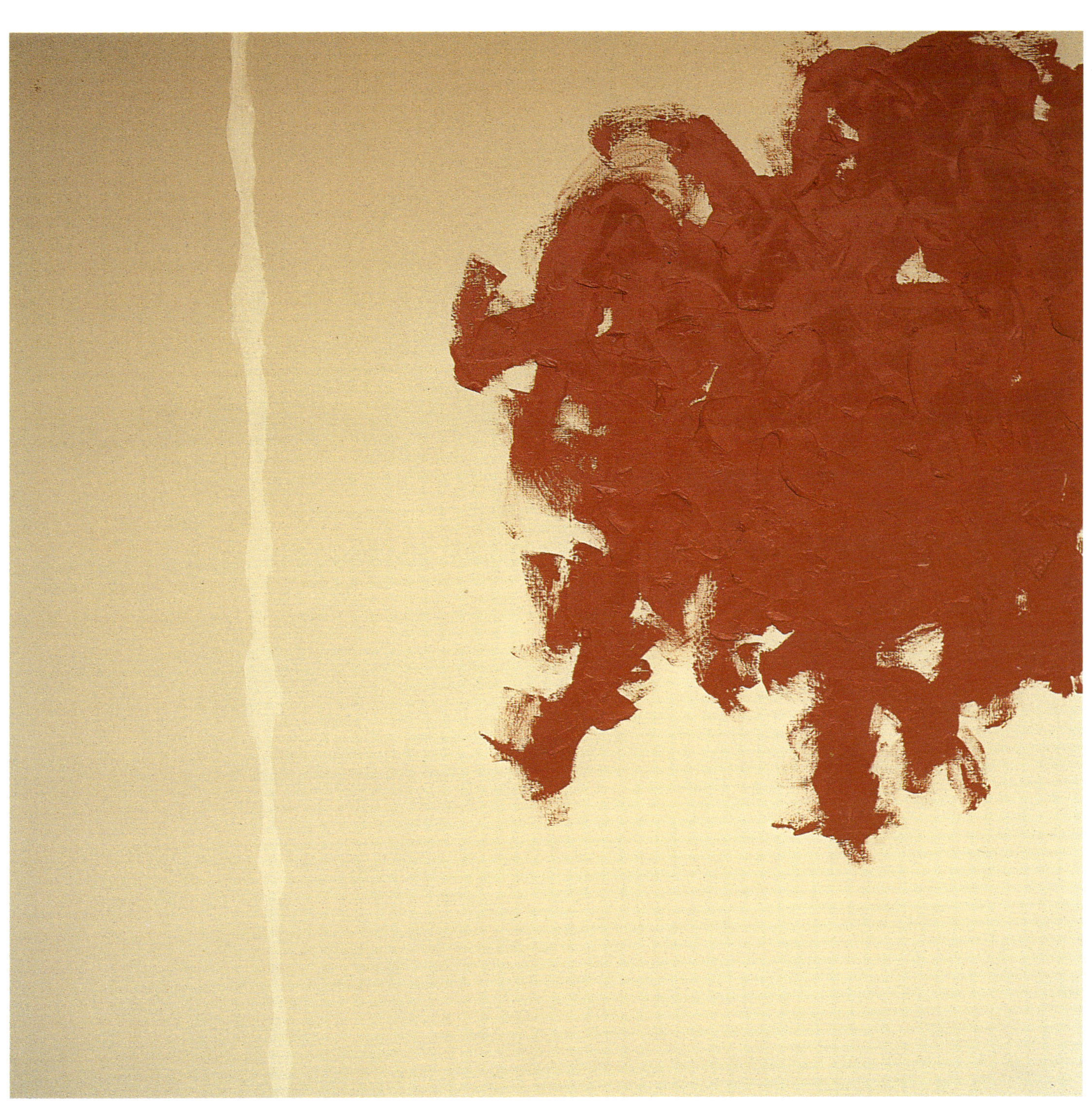

21   15–1958
oil on canvas, 60 x 60 in/152.4 x 152.4 cm. Private collection, London

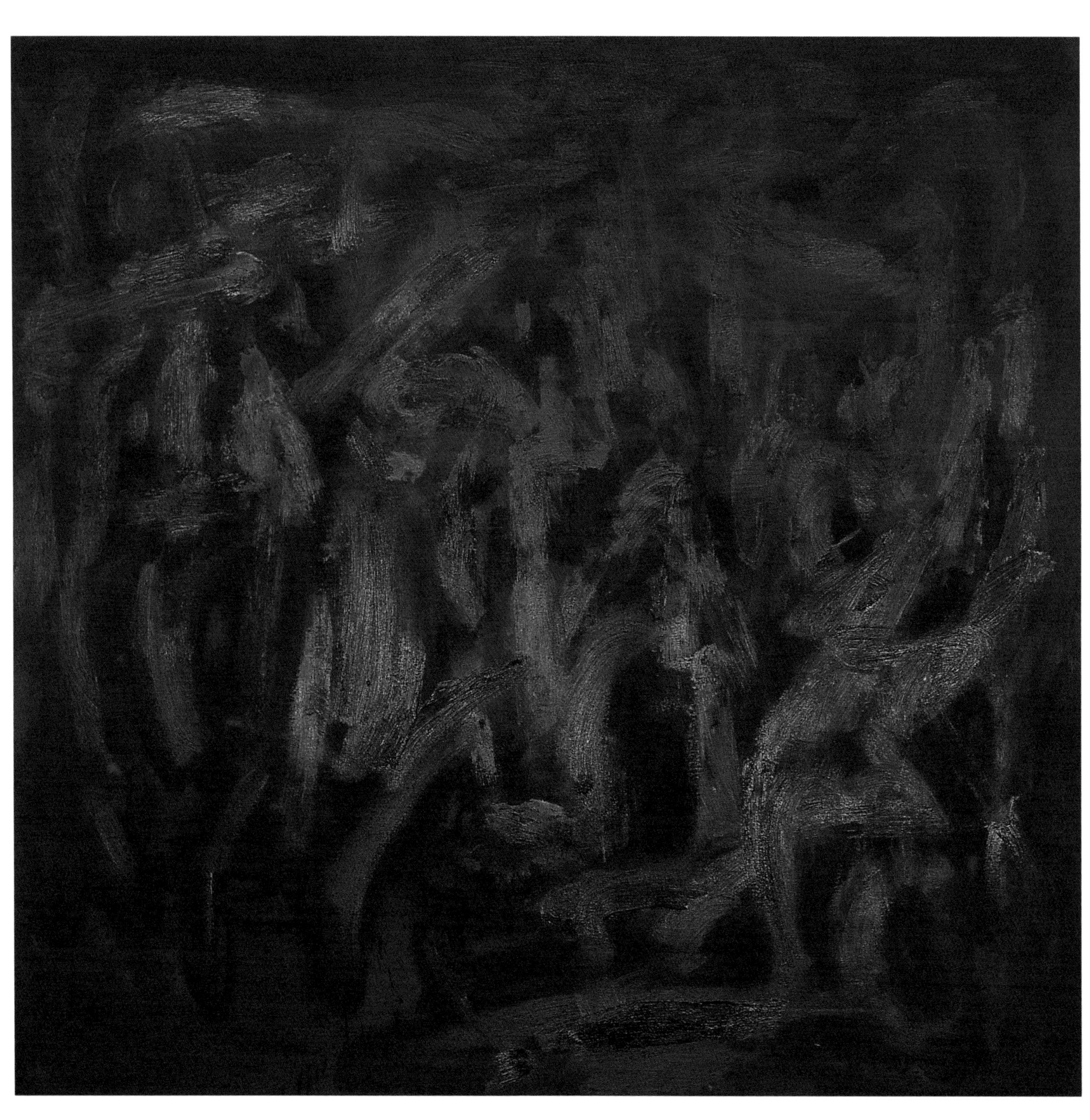

22   3-1958
oil on canvas, 60 x 60 in/152.4 x 152.4 cm. The artist, courtesy Waddington Galleries

23   5-1958
oil on canvas, 60 x 60 in/152.4 x 152.4 cm. The artist, courtesy Waddington Galleries

Gallery in London in the summer of 1956. The exhibition, which also contained work by Richard Hamilton, John McHale, Magda Cordell and Paolozzi among others, has since been accorded a pivotal position in the genesis of the Pop Art movement (despite the fact that the Pop element in the show was minimal). Yet Pop Art's obsession with advertising imagery and consumer culture could hardly be more different from the concerns which informed Turnbull's art, rooted as it was in the archaic and the primitive. Although he was deeply interested in the multifarious aspects of popular media (he had, after all, worked as a magazine illustrator) the idea of making direct appropriations did not appeal. His references to popular culture are, instead, covert and oblique. He does not have the collage mentality which sucks in a great multiplicity of images and reprocesses them in the form of art; rather he has always gathered information in a very discriminating way, being attracted to certain simple, measured forms, whether they occur in ancient art or in contemporary manufactured objects.

Early in 1957 the head motif disappeared from Turnbull's painting and the brushmarks became autonomous, the canvases larger and uniformly coloured (*Painting (black)*, 1957 [plate 17]). His abandonment of figurative content – which was vestigial even in the *Head* paintings – coincided with his first experience of American Abstract Expressionist painting (Pollock's work had featured in the *Opposing Forces* show at the ICA in 1953 but the first representative selection of this new type of painting was in an exhibition held at the Tate Gallery in 1956), and also with his love of Monet's late work. In 1957 Turnbull visited the USA for the first time, and although he met a number of the new generation of abstract painters, including Rothko, he actually saw little of their work. In his sculpture and painting there is a shared concern with surface texture: the energetic brushstrokes of the paintings have their analogue in the corrugated hatchings of the sculptures. Turnbull conceived these paintings as projections of his own self, of his own nature. He put it very lucidly in 1957: ". . . the absorption of nature and the act of painting are two activities reconciled during the act of painting. That is, by projection or extension a dialogue takes place between the artist and his material; and like a conversation it stops when one of the parties involved has nothing more to say to the other. It is impossible to pre-plan – it is a live performance. This is not, as it is often suggested to be, an act of egoism and indifference to nature: rather it is the reverse. It can stem from the deepest respect for things, from the belief that one does not attempt to imitate them or recreate them in their own terms. The artist attempts to create a new object, participating as a parallel activity."[3] These

3. 'Nature into Art', 1957, published in *Uppercase 4*, 1960.

24 25–1959
oil on canvas, 100 x 75 in/254 x 190.5 cm. The artist, courtesy Waddington Galleries

25   7–1958
oil on canvas, 78 x 58 in/198.1 x 147.3 cm. The artist, courtesy Waddington Galleries

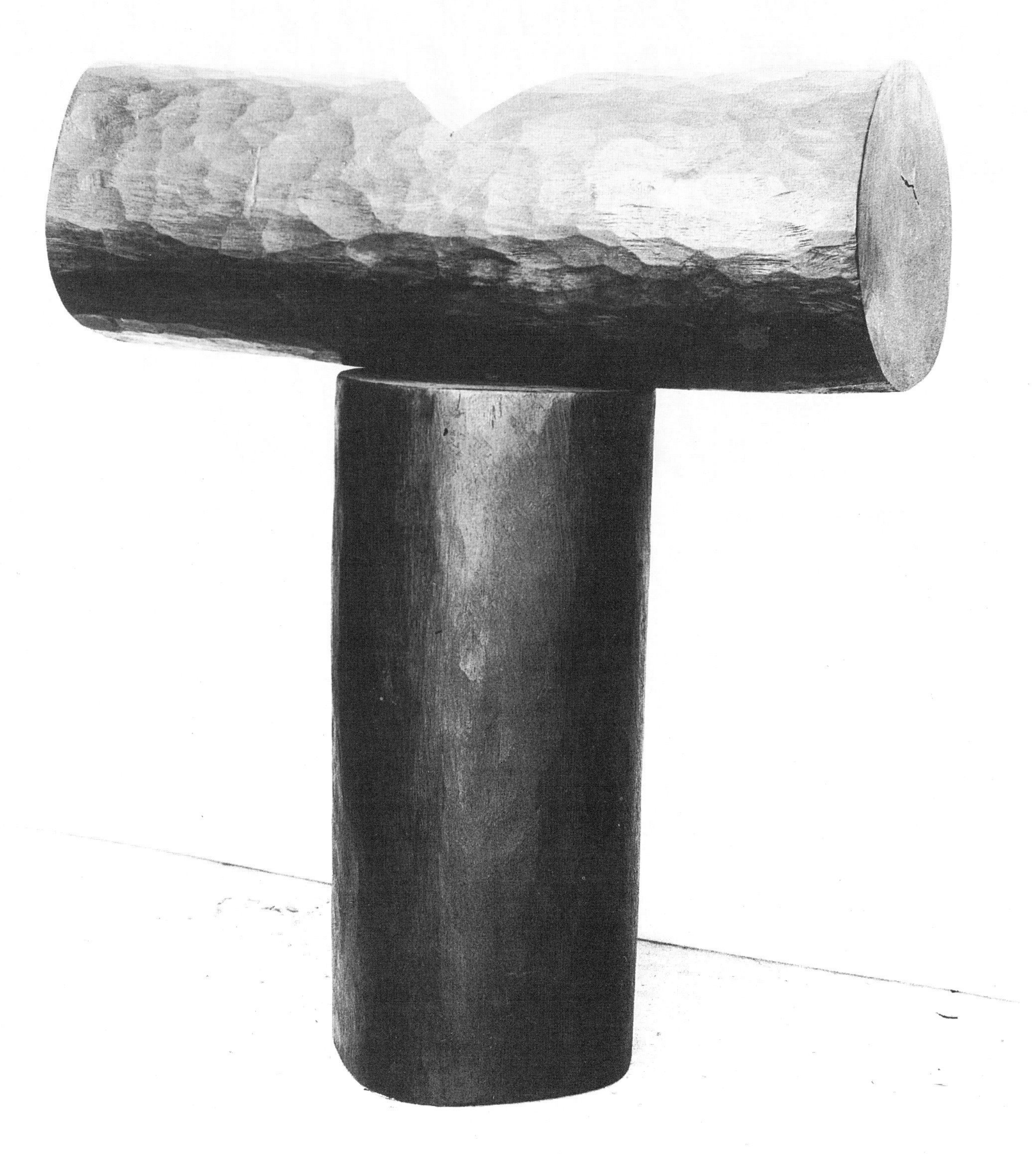

26 Prometheus 1961
rosewood, 37 x 30½ x 12½ in/94 x 77.5 x 31.8cm. Private collection, London

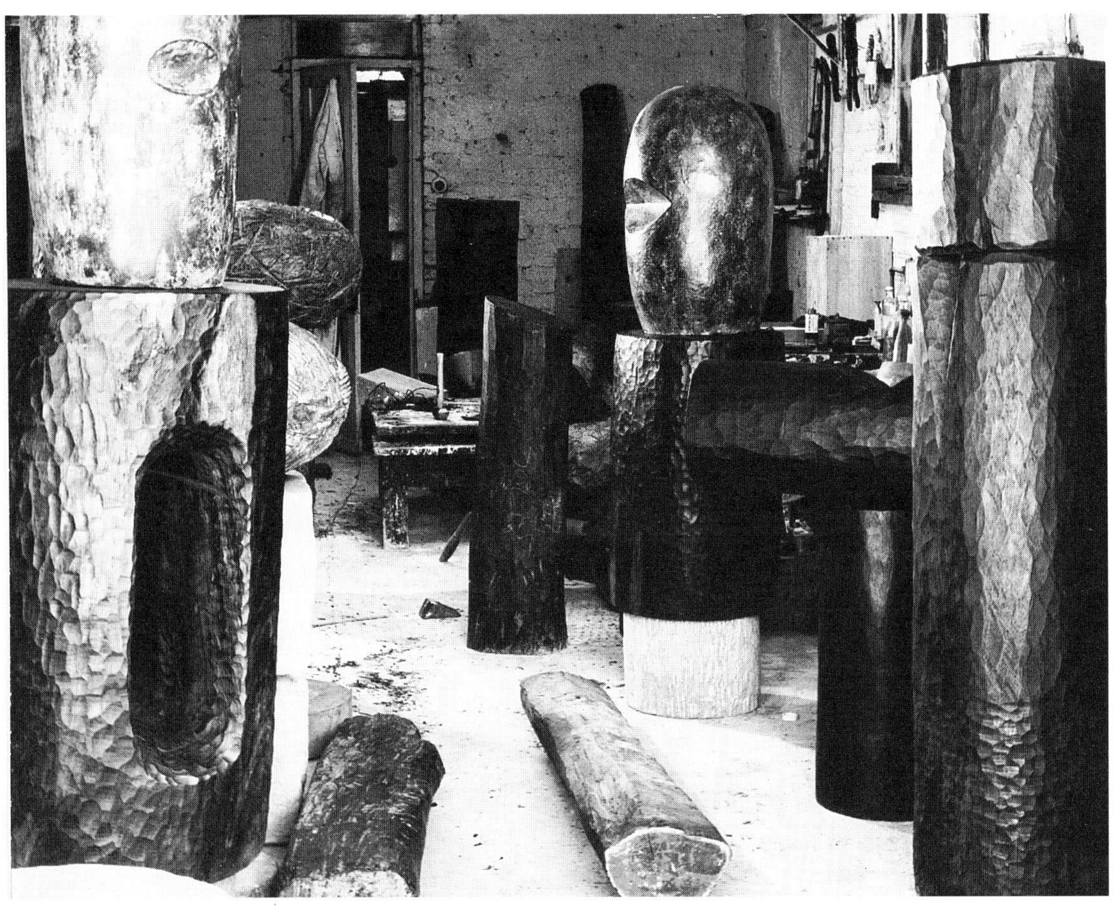

paintings are 'about' colour, shape, surface, but they are also about the act of painting itself. Some of them – and they are among the best paintings made in Britain during that period – are amazingly energetic scrawls of paint on raw, unsized linen (*5–1958* [plate 23]).

By 1957 Turnbull, then in his mid-thirties, was beginning to be acknowledged as one of the finest artists of his generation. His work was, however, difficult to place. It did not belong to a particular group or stylistic tendency and it looked modern and old, figurative and abstract, at the same time. He was known as a sculptor of heads and totemic figures yet he was also making extraordinary, monochromatic paintings. In September he had a solo exhibition of sculpture and painting at the ICA and his work began to sell (in the previous five years he had sold almost no work at all). New sales allowed him to make bronze casts of earlier works which had remained in plaster. While some sculptors will give their plasters to the bronze founder

▷

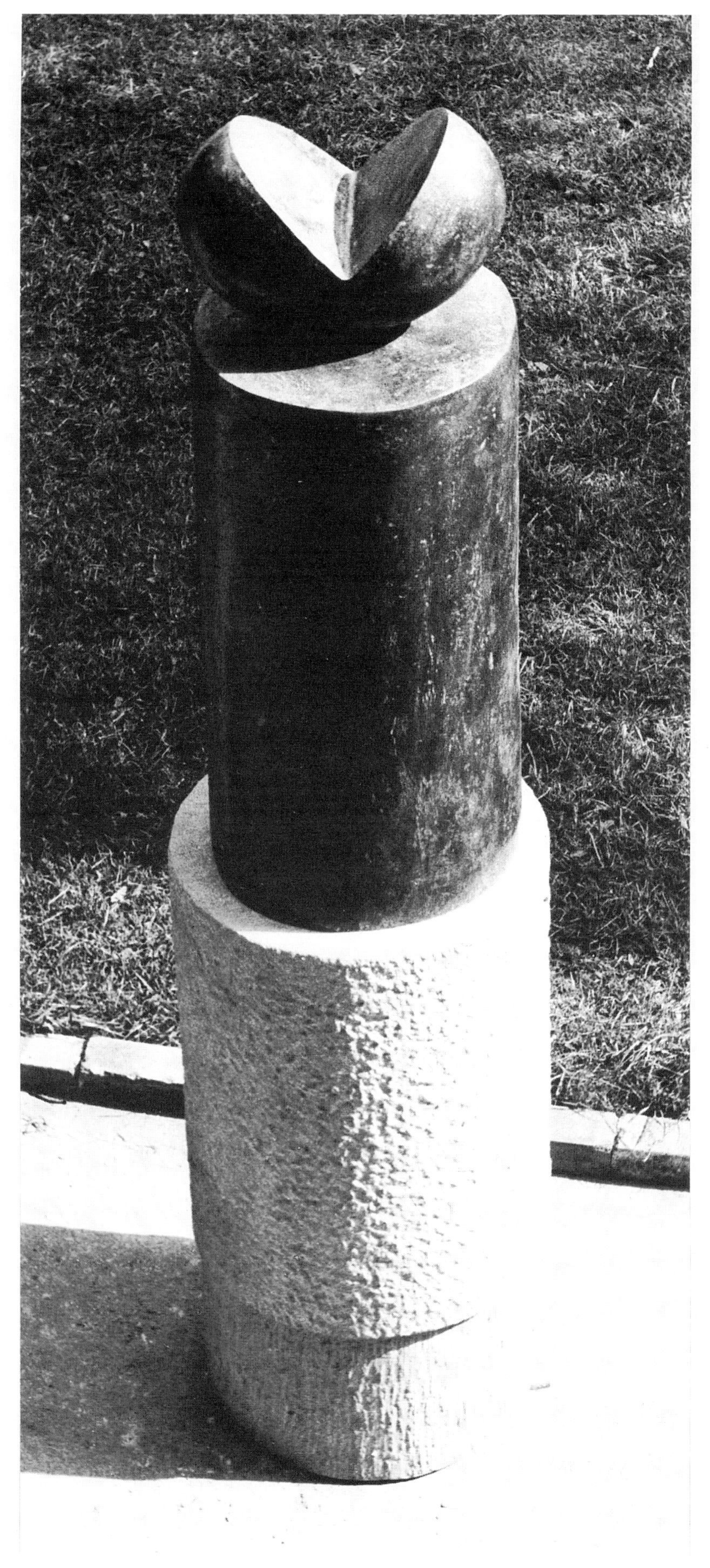

28 Oedipus 2 1962
bronze and stone, 65½ in/166.4 cm high. Private collection, London

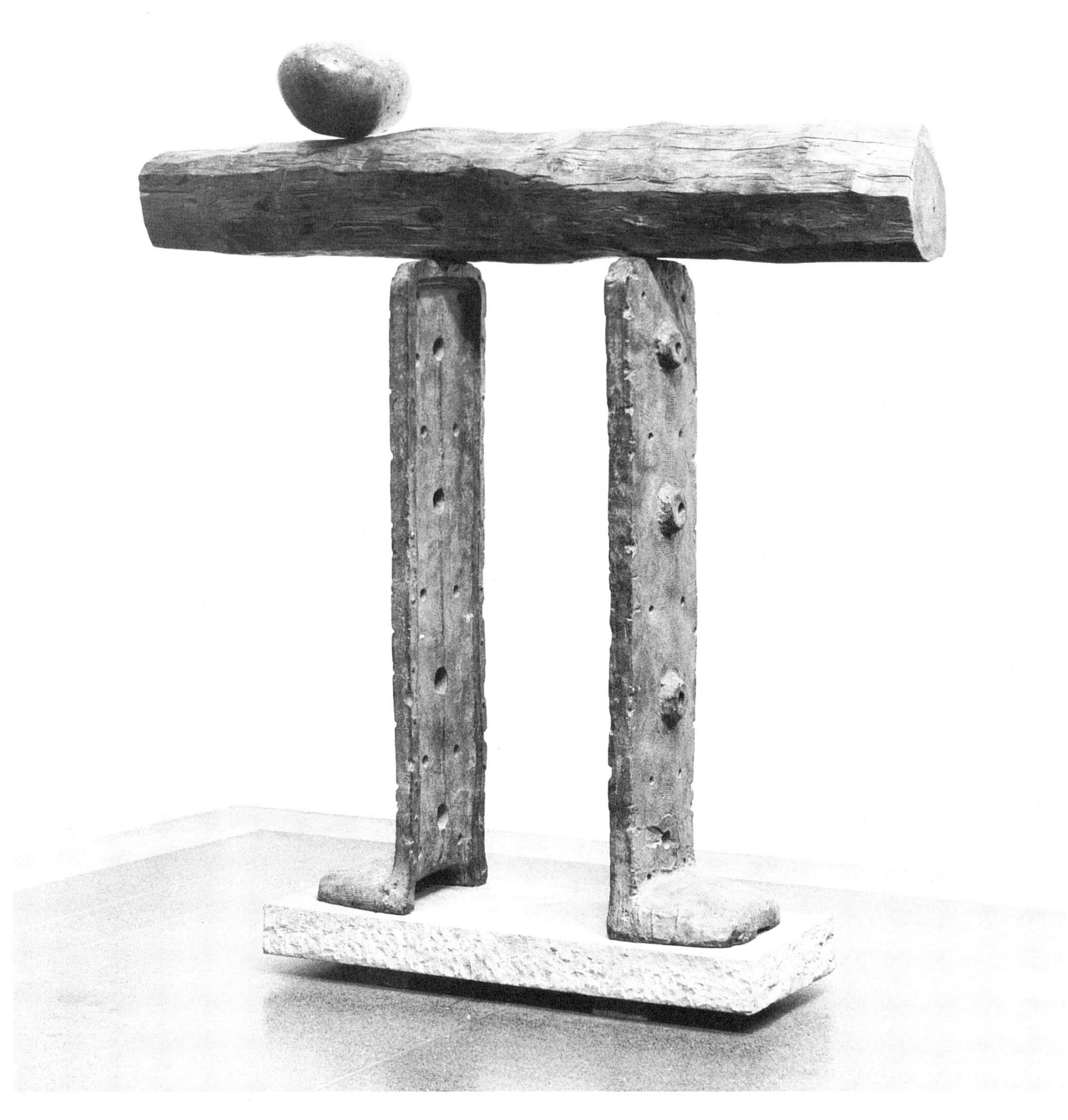

29 Gate 2 1962–63
bronze, rosewood and stone, 82¼ x 73⅝ x 17¾ in/209 x 187 x 45 cm. Scottish National Gallery of Modern Art, Edinburgh

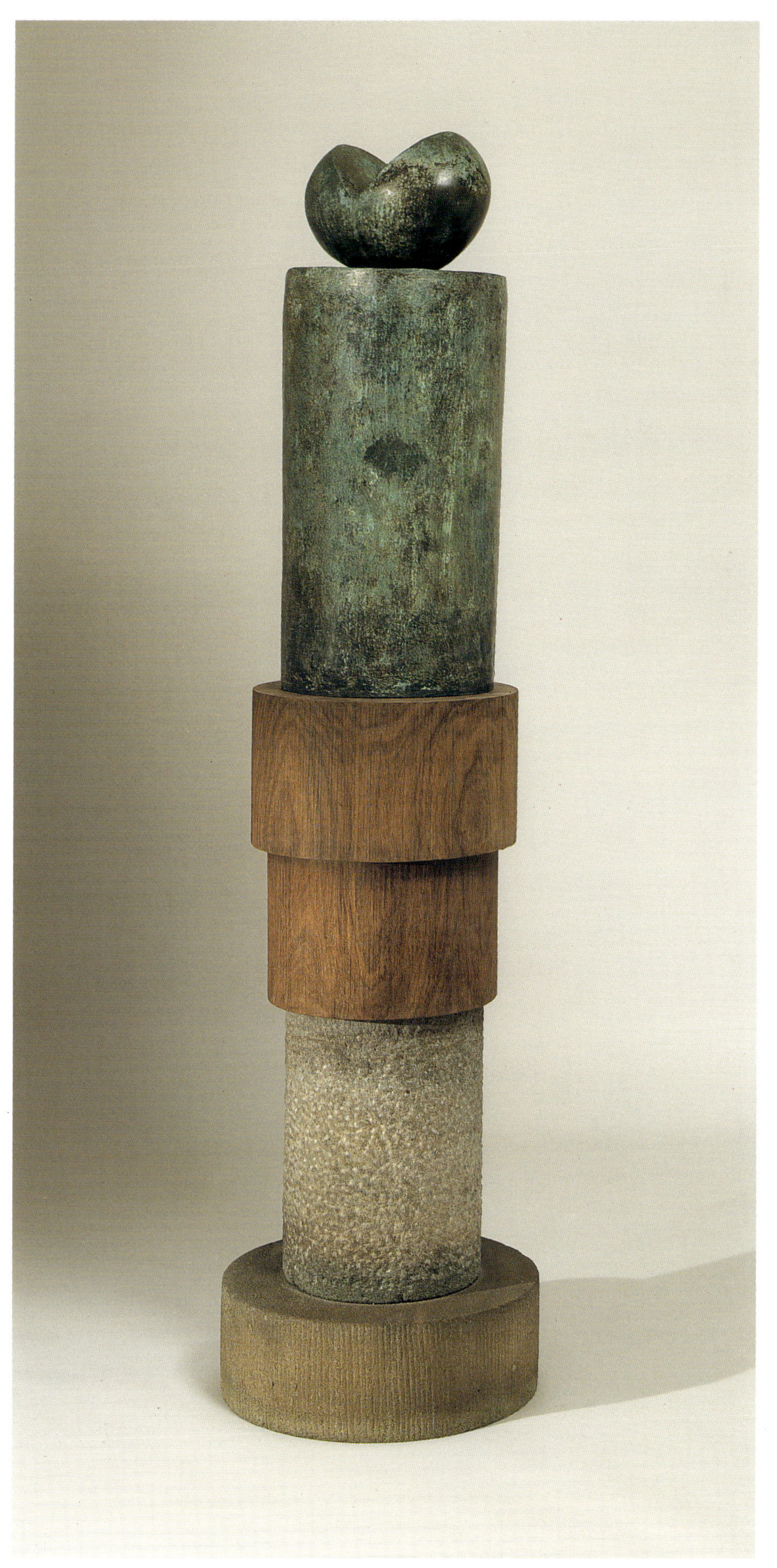

30 Oedipus 3 1962
bronze, rosewood and stone, 76¼ x 19 in diameter/193.7 x 48.3 cm diameter. Private collection, London

and simply take delivery of the casts a few months later, Turnbull has always taken a close interest in the casting process, patinating most works himself. Bronzes were often made by taking a thin gelatin mould of the original plaster sculpture and encasing the gelatin in a rough plaster shell. It was on one of his regular visits to the foundry that Turnbull noticed that the plaster casing used to make another artist's sculpture was characteristic, in an enigmatic and intriguing way, of the sculpture itself. This chance observation led to several evocative works made from the plaster casings of Turnbull's own bronzes. The title of the earliest of these, *Source* of 1958 (plate 18), alludes to its original function as, literally, the source of one of the corrugated female figures made in plaster in 1955 (but only cast three years later). The holes and various marks, which read as strange, possibly magical symbols, are largely functional elements which allowed the gelatin to enter the casing and the air inside to escape. Thus a mundane object was transformed into a metaphorically potent figure, convex on one side and concave on the other, looking like the lid of a sarcophogus or a ritualistic icon one might insert things into. Without being directly imitative of ancient artefacts, Turnbull's work conveys a similar sense of mystery, ritual and awe.

The two-part works in which a horizontal beam is balanced on a tall, totemic form developed into a series of two- and sometimes three-part works: all the sculptures made between 1958 and 1962 featured two or more separate elements stacked one on top of the other. Giacometti had been Turnbull's most important point of reference from the late 1940s, but the multi-part works of the late 1950s are closer in spirit to the work of Brancusi. Just as *Sungazer* had incorporated two elements which had originally been conceived as independent works, so a number of Turnbull's sculptures of the late 1950s were composite structures. The head element of *Aphrodite* (plate 19) of 1958 was conceived a year earlier as an independent work standing on a low stone base, and in works of the early 1960s the head and base elements became partly interchangeable. These permutations were developed in an entirely visual way, being the product of trial, error and experiment. Turnbull has never been interested in theory.

During 1959 his sculpture and painting began to be less concerned with gestural marks and texture and more to do with flat surface. In the bronzes the rough, corrugated surfaces gave way to smooth, rounded forms. Developing from the multi-part sculptures were the sculptures made from a variety of different materials, namely stone, wood and bronze. On a visit

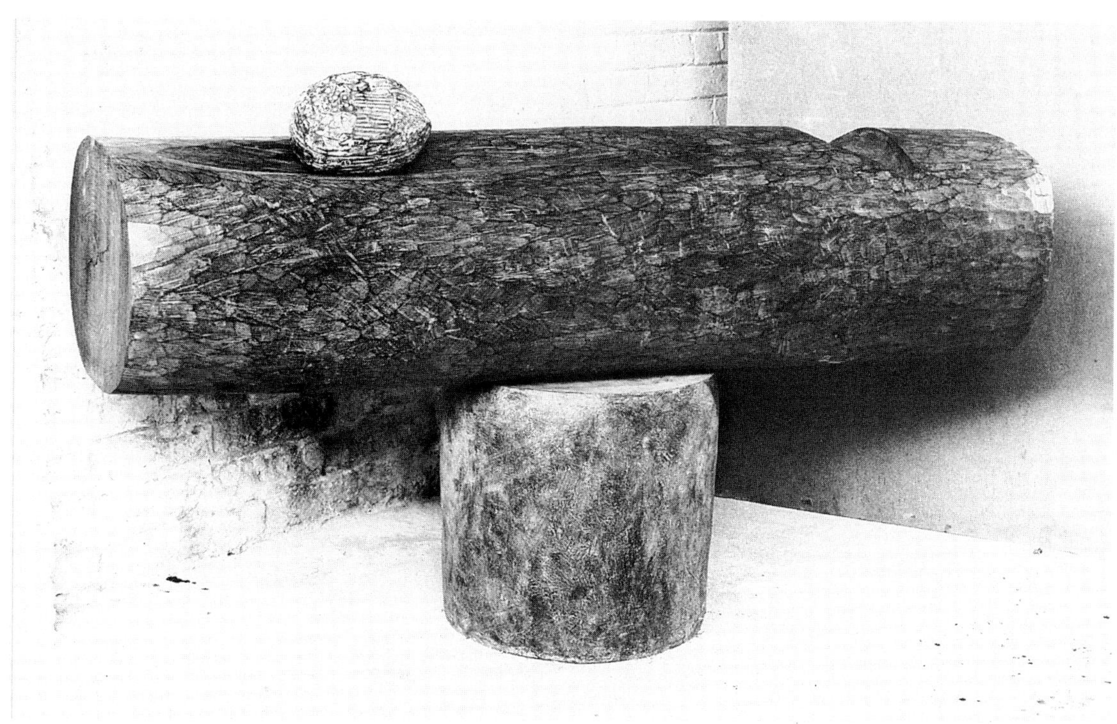

to a timber merchant in north London, Turnbull chanced upon a stack of large rosewood logs – a rare find even in those days – and bought the lot. He had used wooden dowels and boards in a few early works but had not previously done any carving. Now he began to carve the logs, altering their form only minimally, as in the haunting *Chief* (visible on the extreme right of the studio photograph, plate 27) of 1962, which has a simple V-shaped wedge cut out of it, and in *Oedipus* 3 (plate 30), also of 1962, which is composed of a number of stacked bronze, wood and stone elements. The stone parts were generally found at stonemasons' yards and were, like the rosewood, used in a hardly altered form. As in Brancusi's work, the traditional division between sculpture and base is eliminated: it is not possible to say where the base stops and where the sculpture begins because the two are united. The sliced-egg form, which featured on top of the three tall *Oedipus* sculptures (*e.g. Oedipus* 2 [plate 28]) and in their more reticent cousin, the floor-hugging *Lotus*, developed from Turnbull's fascination with opening flowers and was inspired by Monet's *Nymphée* paintings. The problem of how to suggest the delicacy and semi-transparency of an opening water-lily in bronze intrigued Turnbull and

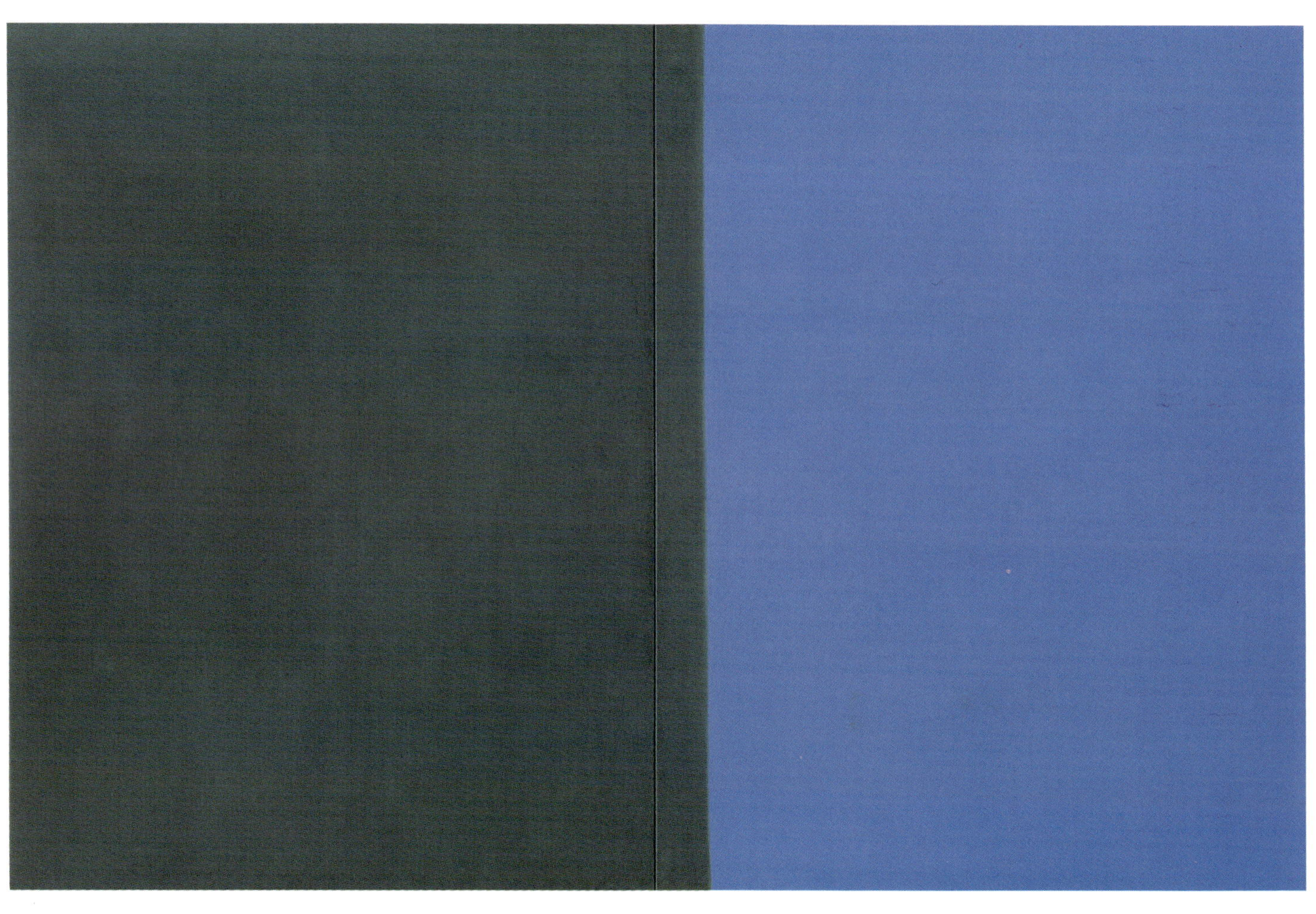

32   1–1962

oil on canvas, 2 canvases, each 100 x 74 in/254 x 188 cm. Tate Gallery, London

resulted in this form which reappears in other works of the period. The cut sphere of the flower also reads as a head looking upwards (like *Sungazer*), hence the title *Oedipus*, after the tragic figure of Greek legend who blinded himself by staring into the sun.

The paintings of the late 1950s and early 1960s became increasingly large. Whereas before he had used a palette knife to emphasize texture, now he painted in layers with a brush, achieving such a rich, chromatic quality that it was difficult to gauge where the surface of the picture lay. Turnbull conceived his paintings as a kind of environmental art, art on such a vast scale that it enveloped the viewer and became an experience in itself rather than an imitation of something else. The experience of the painting changed, depending on how near one stood to it: close to they have an almost hypnotic presence. Some of the paintings of the late 1950s still retain the circle form found in the earlier *Head* paintings, though here the motif has become disembodied. Others, particularly those of the early 1960s, are in two colours, divided vertically near the middle. The effect is very expansive, as if the axis extended beyond the edge of the canvas. In the same way that some of the sculptures had direct if hidden references to aspects of popular culture, so did the paintings, for the broad, horizontal ones are like Cinemascope screens. Turnbull often sat in the front row at the cinema so that the image was enormous and enveloped him. A panoramic image in a Spencer Tracy film (*Bad Day at Black Rock*), in which a train snakes across a vast, empty desert, is reformulated in some of the paintings, though generally it was the overwhelming size of the screen that impressed him. In 1953 Turnbull had even made two films, one of which showed a still shot of the colour red heating up under the projector and eventually blistering and burning. Like the paintings and sculpture this film commented on the process of its own making and identity. Other paintings respond to the aerial views of the jungle and rivers of the Far East. In 1960 Turnbull exhibited some of the largest of his paintings with the Situation Group at the Royal British Architects Gallery. Other participants included Bernard Cohen, Robyn Denny, Gordon House and Gillian Ayres, and all the works were at least 30 square foot in size.

In 1960 Turnbull and the artist Kim Lim were married and in the winter of 1962–63 they travelled to Japan, Cambodia and her native Singapore. Turnbull was struck by the many formal gates one had to pass through to enter and exit religious sites, and in particular was impressed by the way each gate framed, altered and conditioned the space in a different way. On his visit to the museums in New York he had observed a similar device used by Matisse, whose paintings often feature open windows: these windows establish a dialogue between inside and outside spaces. Turnbull's response was to make a series of gate sculptures (they also read as altars). *Gate* 2 (plate 29) of 1962–63, is one of the largest and most complex of the multi-part, multi-media works, featuring a stone base, bronze casts of the front and back halves of the plaster casing used to make *Screwhead*, and a rosewood bar supporting a bronze head made some years earlier. The base rests on unseen wooden bars, so that the entire structure appears to float above the ground. This effort seemingly to evade gravity, to make forms such as the lotus-flower appear as if they are light and floating, pervades Turnbull's sculpture and painting of these years.

The work of the early 1960s involved less and less hand-crafting, the wood and stone components scarcely differing from their found state. In 1963 he made a sculpture, *No.1*, which was basically a vertical cylinder with a shorter, flat element projecting from the top at a slight angle. This had been made in wood which was then cast in bronze and turned on a lathe to produce a very regular machine-made finish. A series of related works followed, but instead of casting them from wooden originals he made them directly in steel. In 1963 Turnbull had been offered a full-time post as Head of Sculpture at the Central School (he had stopped teaching his other course in 1961), but had turned it down in favour of a two-day-a-week post which he took up the following year. The man he recommended for the job instead, Brian Wall, taught him how to do electric arc-welding and Turnbull subsequently ordered pre-manufactured cylindrical steel components which he cut and welded. A few sculptors had begun to use steel in the 1950s and early 1960s, notably the American sculptor David Smith and the British sculptor Anthony Caro. Welded steel offered a very direct, creative way of working which was neither modelling nor carving. Unlike cast bronze, steel bars can be long, thin and very strong, and welded together they can create expansive, open forms; moreover steel can easily be painted, and colour adds to the sense of weightlessness.

The change of materials in Turnbull's sculpture, from the warmth of wood and bronze, which betray the original touch of the carver's or modeller's hand, to the cold finish of machine-made steel, was a significant one, but the development was consistent with the work that had gone before. Just as Turnbull's works of the early 1960s were composed of a number of different elements joined together, so it was not a totally new departure when he took pieces of steel and began to weld them together. Formally, too, there are many similarities: works such

▷

33   12–1963
oil on canvas, 40 x 40 in/101.6 x 101.6 cm. The artist, courtesy Waddington Galleries

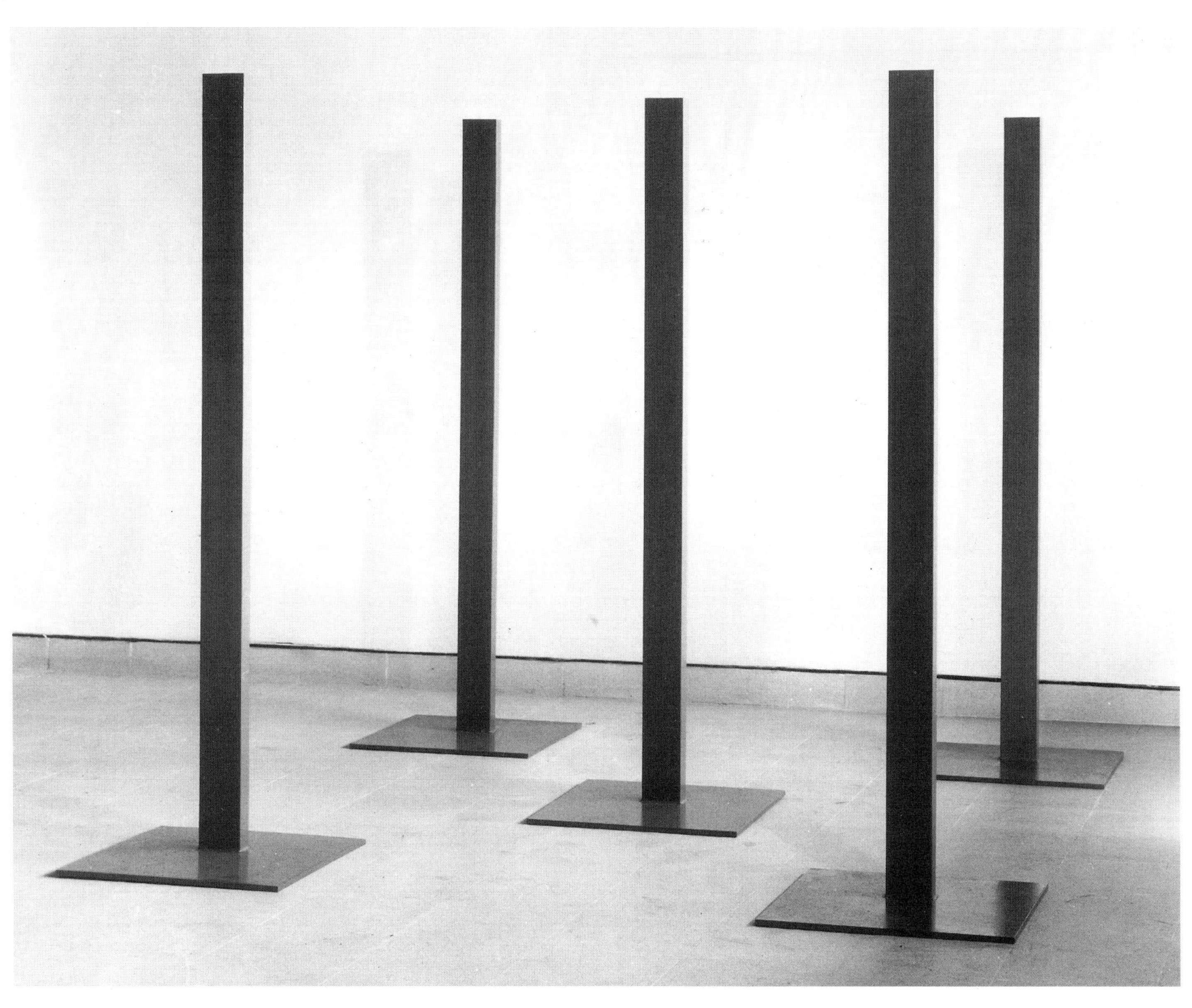

34　5 x 1–1966
steel painted Thames green, each 72½ x 22 x 21 in/184.2 x 55.9 x 53.3 cm. Tate Gallery, London

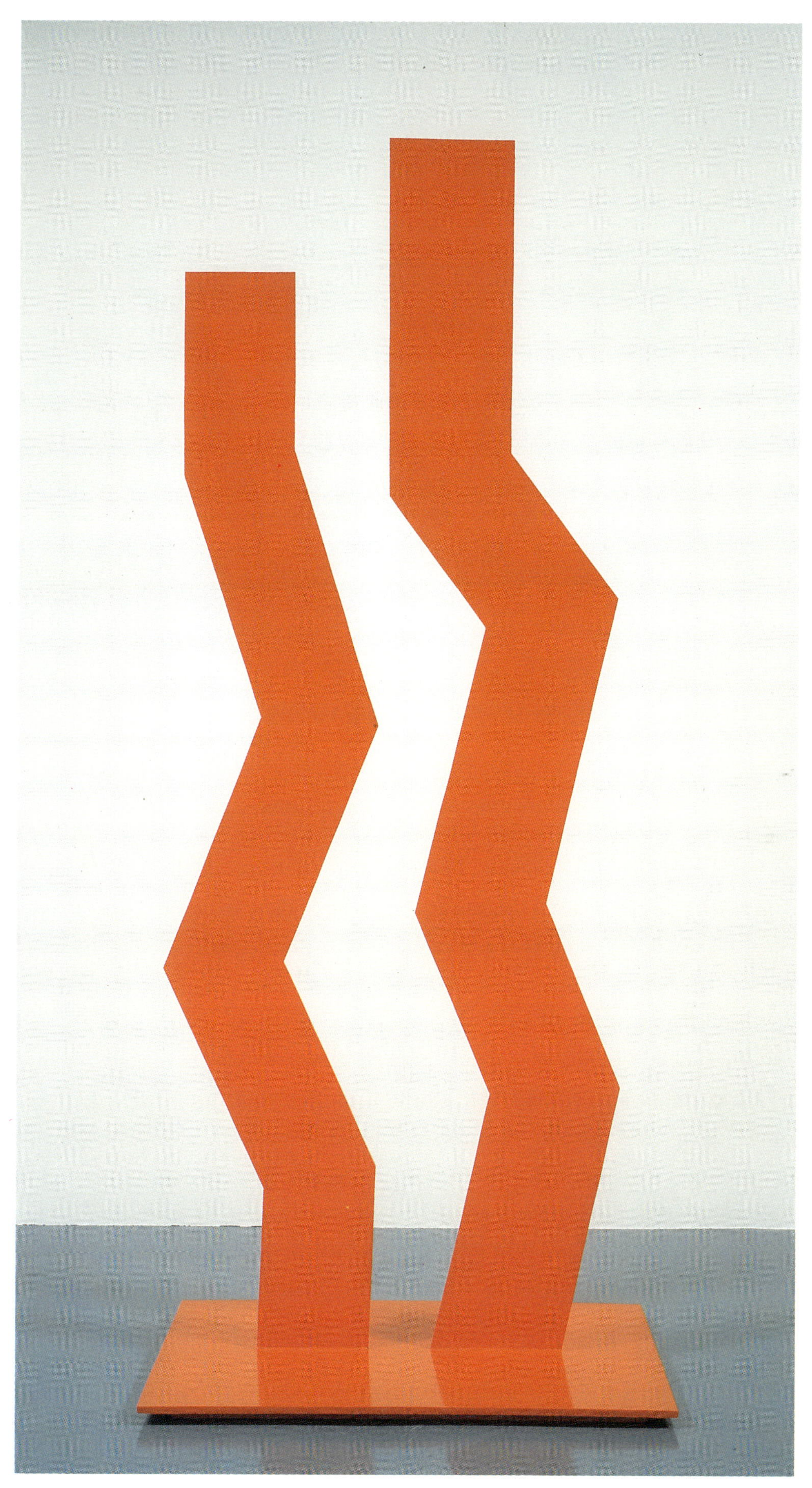

35 Double red 1966
steel painted red, 90 x 25 x 36in/228.6 x 63.5 x 91.4cm. The British Council

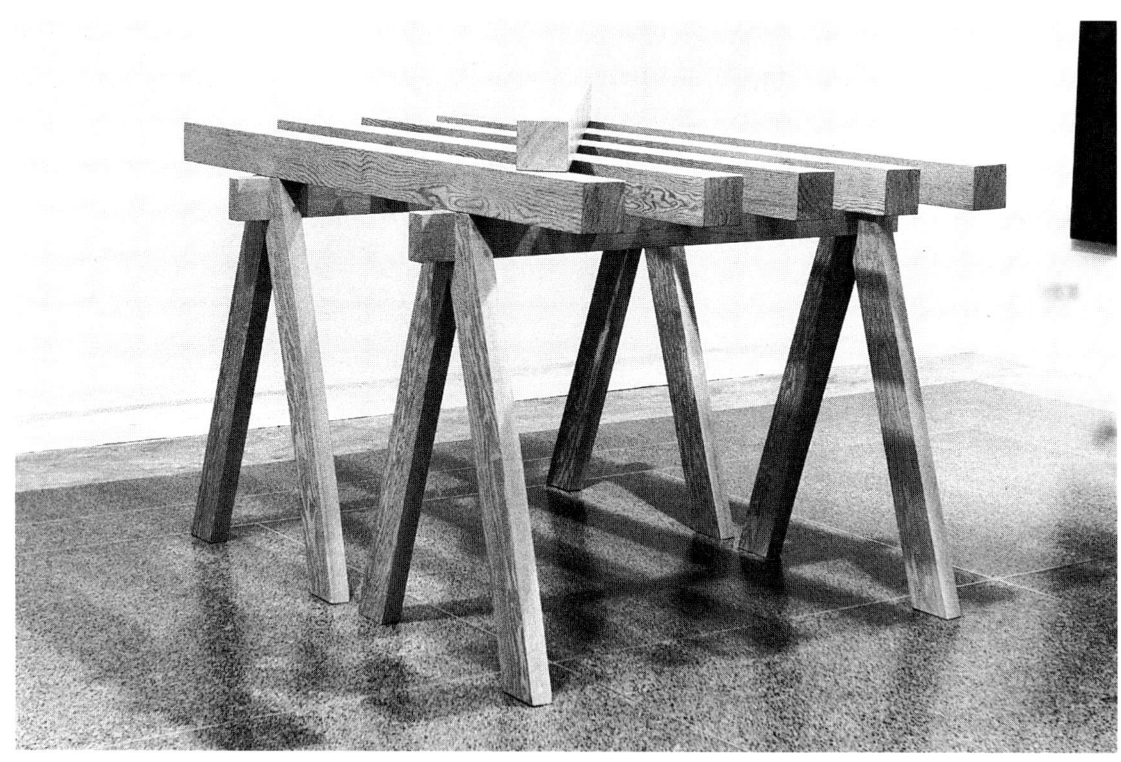

as *Double red* (plate 35) of 1966 continue the gate form developed in the early 1960s. The work remained decidedly frontal and totemic. This was quite different from the work of Smith and Caro, whose sculpture projected into space in a more three-dimensional way, encouraging the viewer to walk around it and observe it from different angles. Even in painting the sculptures Turnbull was returning to a practice he had adopted twenty years earlier when at the Slade he had painted *Horse* a bright yellow.

Just as Turnbull had hardly altered the form of the rosewood log to make a work such as *Chief*, so it was that he scarcely altered the form of the components he ordered for his steel works. In all these works there is a discreet response to the material, a desire not to interfere with its integrity. It is almost as if, were wood and steel able to make sculpture out of themselves, they would make works like these. Works such as *Triple* and *Laocoon* grow out of the ground in an apparently natural way, as if they had not been mediated by an artist. These works are 'about' the material in the same way that the paintings are 'about' colour; and they

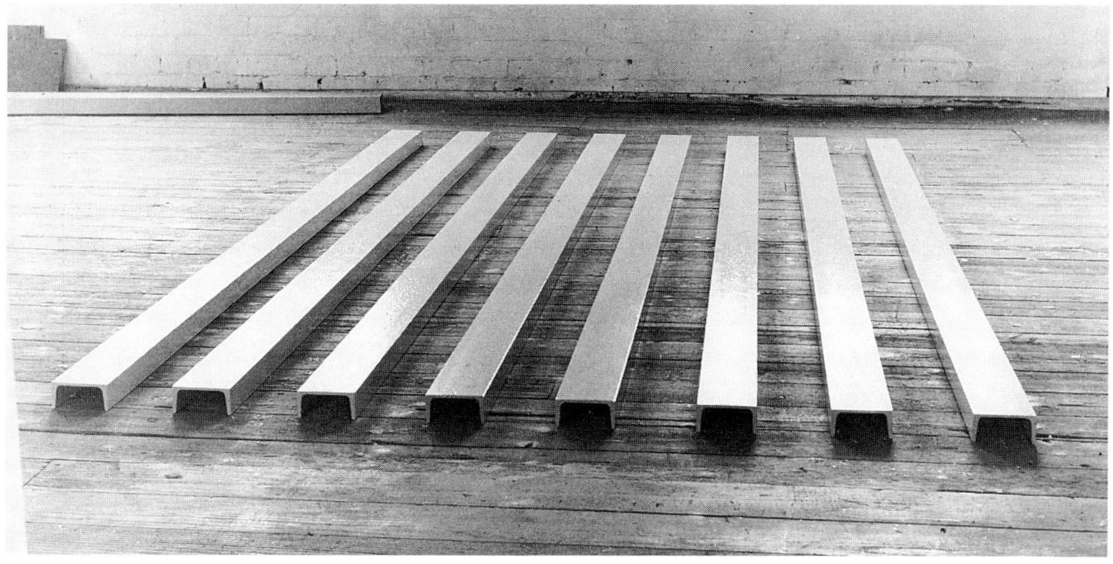

are perceptual rather than conceptual or theoretical works, acting on the viewer in a direct way. As Turnbull remarked at the time, his works were to do with experience rather than ideas: we do not need screeds of documentation in order to respond to them. Through minimal manipulation Turnbull transformed banal materials into new kinds of experiences.

In 1966 Turnbull ordered a batch of angled steel beams, each four-and-a-half foot in length. It was only after welding three of them together, to form three edges of a cube, that he saw the potential for making five modular variations, each describing the parameters of a partially formed cube. Grouped together the six elements became *Sextet* (plate 38). The Tate Gallery's *5 x 1* developed in a similar way (plate 34). Like *Sextet* it can be arranged in any number of permutations, effectively changing the space it occupies according to the arrangement. Thus the vertical 'figures' can be closed up to create a kind of barrier or can be spaced out to enable the viewer to walk between them. In this way the sculpture affects the way the viewer perceives and experiences the space he or she is moving in – a sensation which relates to that achieved in the earlier monochrome paintings. The emphasis on the floor and on the relationship between the work of art and the space it and the viewer occupy would be a feature of much sculpture made in Britain from the late 1960s. But in a way it was a concern Turnbull had addressed in the late 1940s in his *Game* (plate 2) and *Forms on a base* works, for these were conceived as projects for much larger, room-sized installations.

Most of the steel works are linear in form. They are either emphatically vertical or emphatically horizontal, springing upwards out of the ground or lying across it. *Duct* and *Steps* (plate 41) are exceptions and are more object-like. *Duct*, 1966, is in the form of an air duct, sealed at the top and finished with an electric rotating polisher. The result is a beautifully self-contained, autonomous object. A few years later he made several other object-sculptures, including a trestle table (plate 36), which almost exactly copied the form of such tables, but which is a paradigm of measured and evenly balanced forms. Such works were on the very fringes of what, at the time, could be considered sculpture.

The so called 'New' British sculpture that emerged out of the St Martin's School of Art from the late 1960s – the work of Richard Long, Barry Flanagan and Bruce McLean, for example – is usually seen as a reaction to the welded metal sculpture of artists such as Turnbull and Caro, and in a sense it was. Nevertheless, the work of this generation owed an immense amount to their forebears, particularly to the way in which works such as *Sextet* were conceived

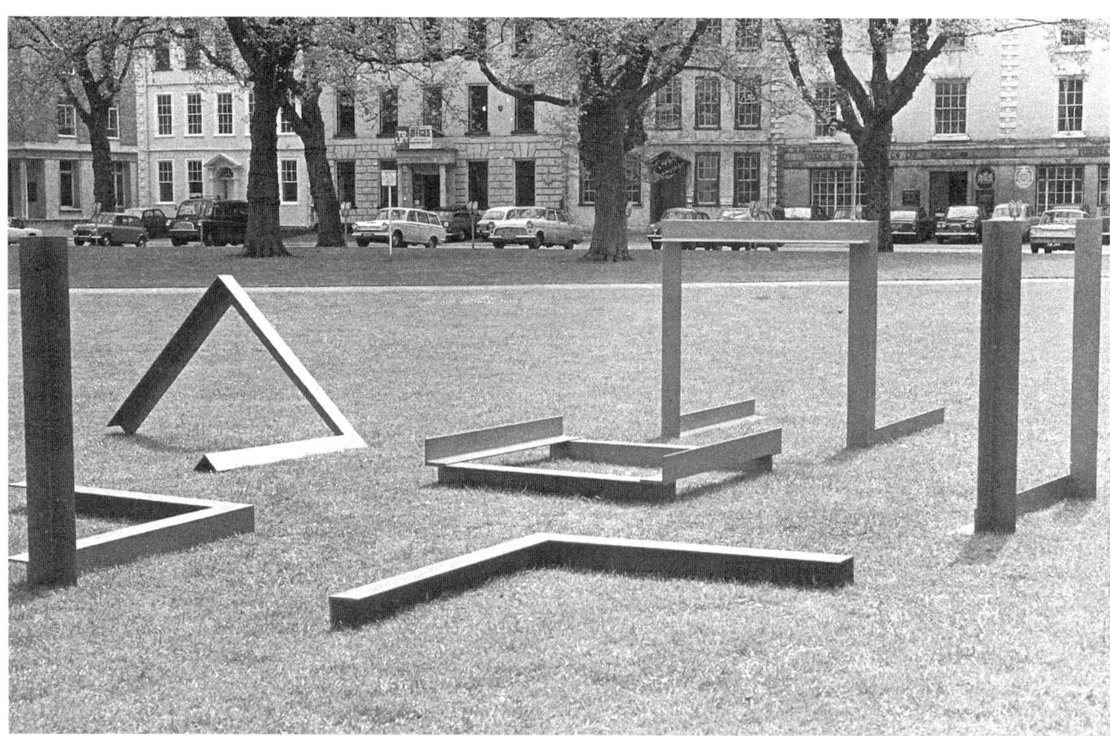

38
Sextet 1966–67
steel painted red; each
sculpture made of
54 in/137.2 cm
lengths of 5 x 5 angle
Waddington Galleries,
London

not as precious, 'artistic' forms to be placed on a plinth but as factual, object-like structures which occupied landscape settings; and also in the way in which such sculptures, made from 'found' materials, were not immutable but could be shifted about. From 1966 to 1968 Turnbull made some remarkable works which address many of the concerns which would preoccupy the younger generation. For example, *One* of 1966 was simply an eighteen-foot-long, painted steel beam placed on the floor. *Parallels* of 1967 (plate 37) was a row of nine-foot-long steel lengths placed on the floor and painted different colours. Turnbull also began to work in transparent plastics. *Corrugations* 2, 1967, consists of a number of the pre-fabricated, corrugated plastic sheets for temporary roofing placed against the wall around the artist's studio, while *Wattle* of 1971 is a set of six ready-made wattle fence units which can be placed in any number of ways, whether piled on top of each other or stuck into the ground in a formal composition. Assembled together in Turnbull's studio in Southey Road, north London, the works and the space seemed to join together to form one vast artwork. ▷

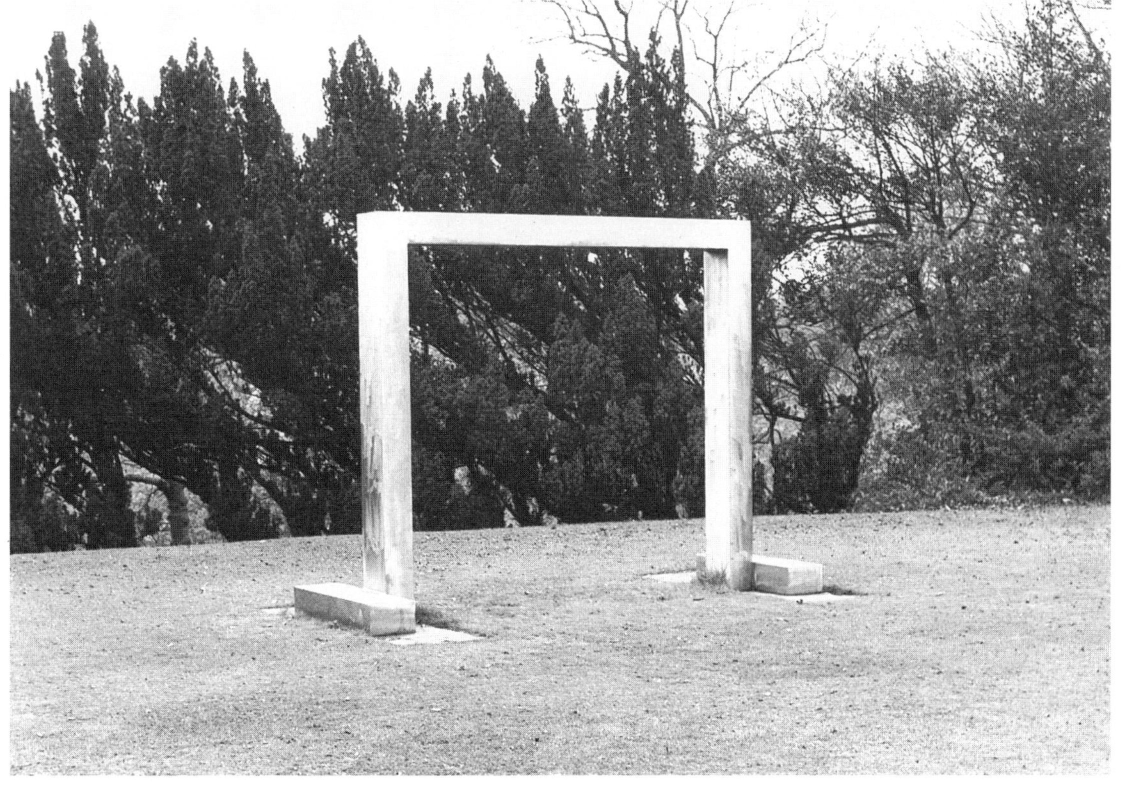

39
Gate 1972
stainless steel
85½ x 115 x 36 in/
217.2 x 292.1 x
91.4 cm
Scottish National
Gallery
of Modern Art,
Edinburgh

40   13–1968
oil on canvas, 70 x 70 in/177.8cm x 177.8 cm. The artist, courtesy Waddington Galleries

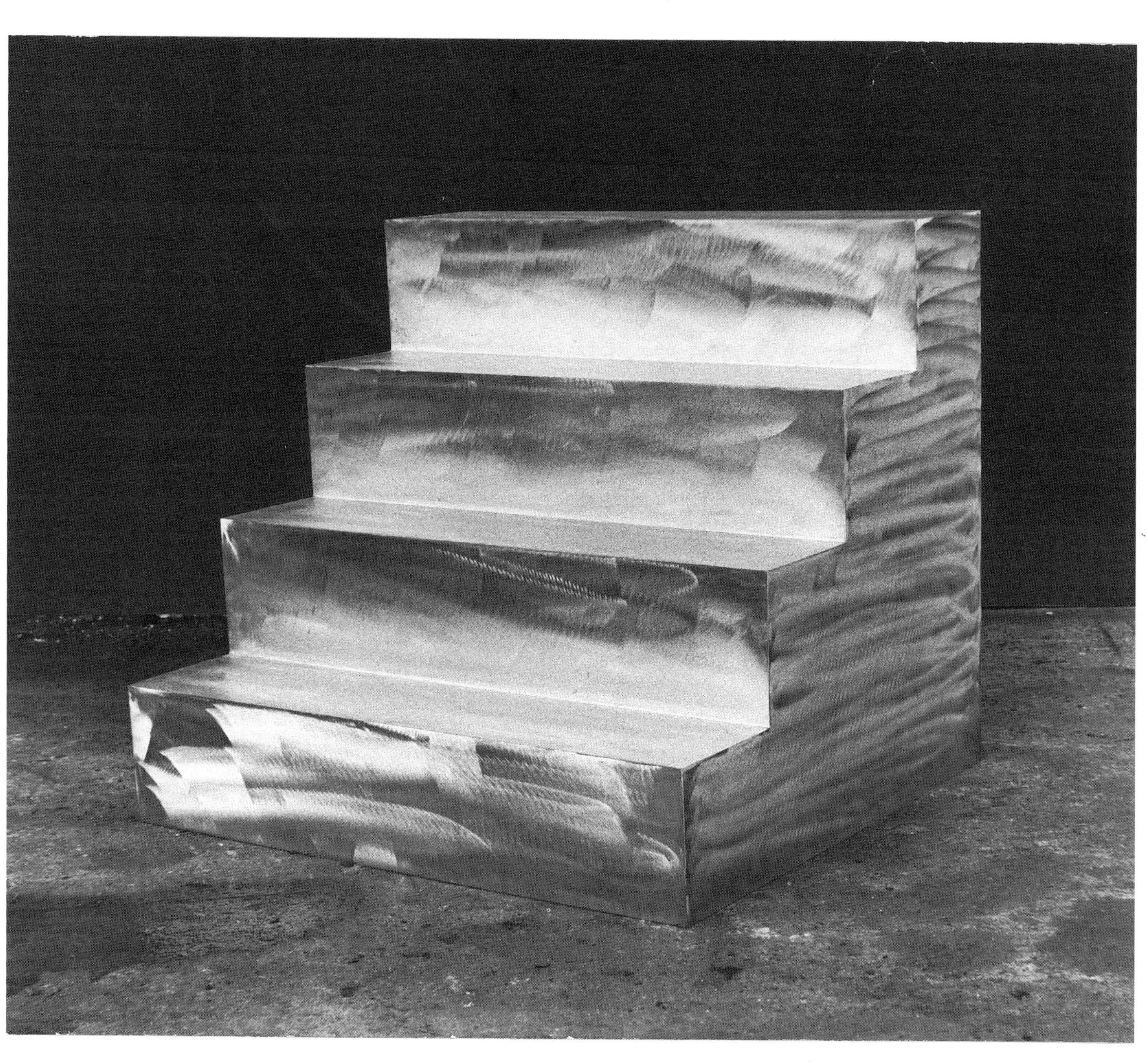

41 Steps 1967–72
stainless steel, 36 x 36 x 40 in/91.4 x 91.4 x 101.6 cm. Tehran Museum of Contemporary Art, Iran

42   3-1976

oil on canvas, 70 x 70in/177.8 x 177.8cm. The artist, courtesy Waddington Galleries

43   11–1976

oil on canvas, 70 x 70 in/177.8 x 177.8 cm. The artist, courtesy Waddington Galleries

44 13-1976
oil on canvas, 60 x 60 in/152.4 x 152.4 cm. The artist, courtesy Waddington Galleries

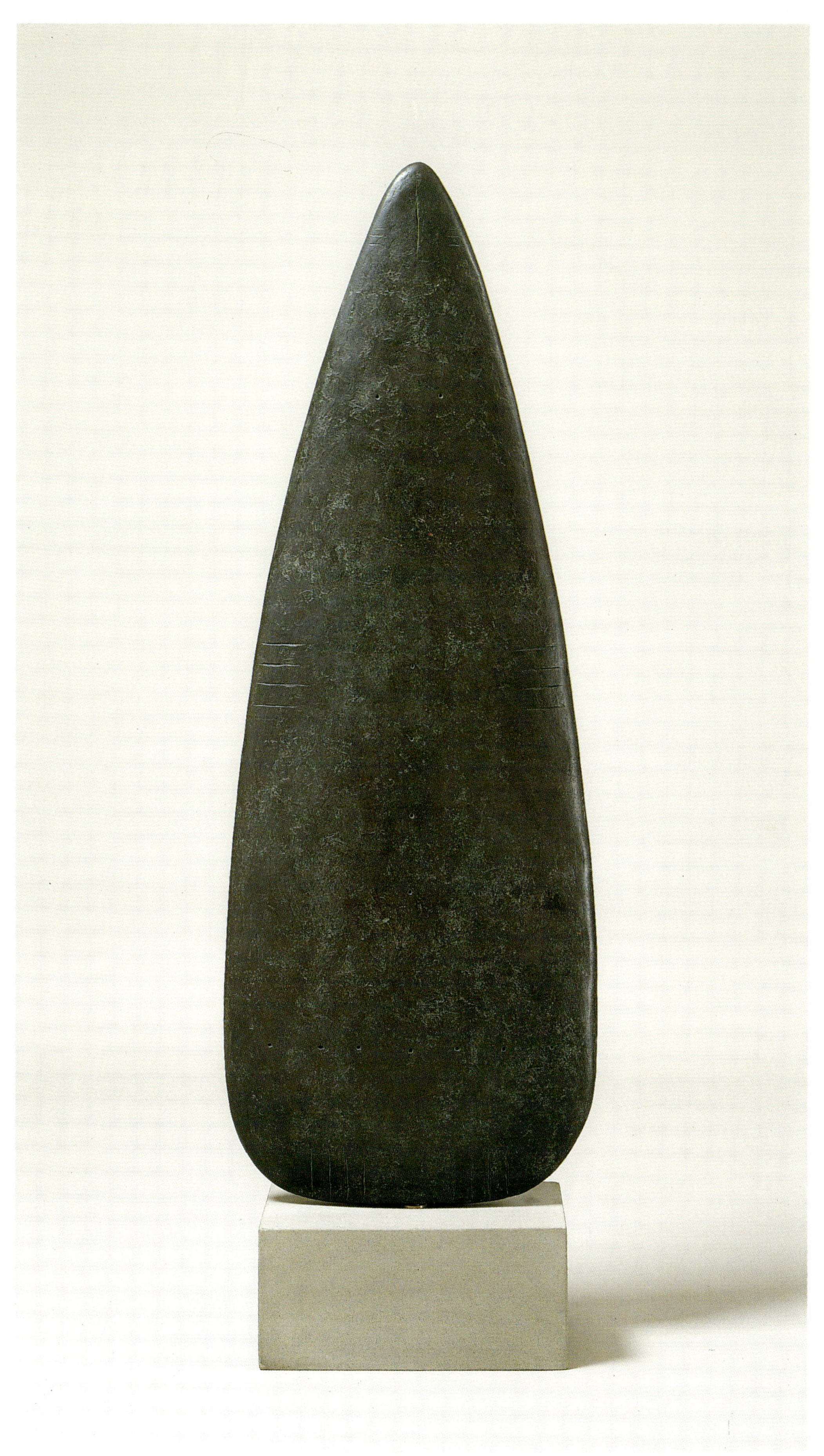

45 Leaf Venus 2 1986, bronze on stone base, bronze 46 x 16½ x 3 in/
116.8 x 41.9 x 7.6 cm, base 6 x 11½ x 7½/15.2 x 29.2 x 19 cm. Edition of 4 plus 1 artist's copy. The artist, courtesy Waddington Galleries

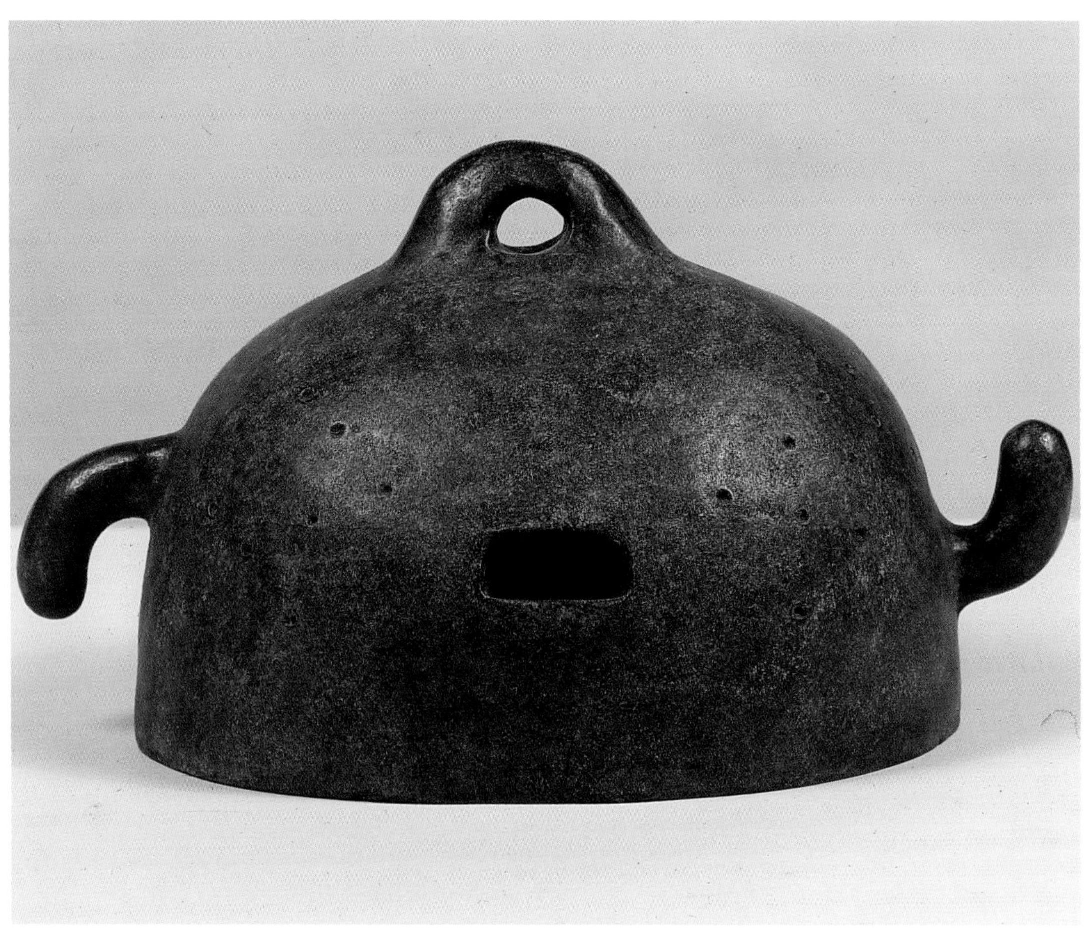

The paintings from the mid-1960s were of uniform colour but often had differently coloured stripes placed discreetly at the edges. In one series he used a colour which exactly duplicated the colour of the bare canvas and in another left the canvas almost completely bare, save for a thin strip of colour at the bottom. Some of the canvases were enormous – nearly twenty feet long. Once more, the paintings connect quite closely with the contemporaneous sculpture. Just as a sculpture such as *One* was a pre-fabricated piece of metal which Turnbull simply painted, so the canvases are similarly discrete objects composed of canvas on stretcher which Turnbull painted in single colours. Reinforcing the three-dimensional, 'object' nature of the paintings, he would often paint the sides of the canvas and prop the works up against the wall rather than hang them in the conventional way.

In 1973 Turnbull had a retrospective exhibition at the Tate Gallery: it filled the large central galleries and ranged from the student work of the 1940s to the steel sculptures of the early 1970s. Seeing all the paintings and sculptures displayed together made him highly

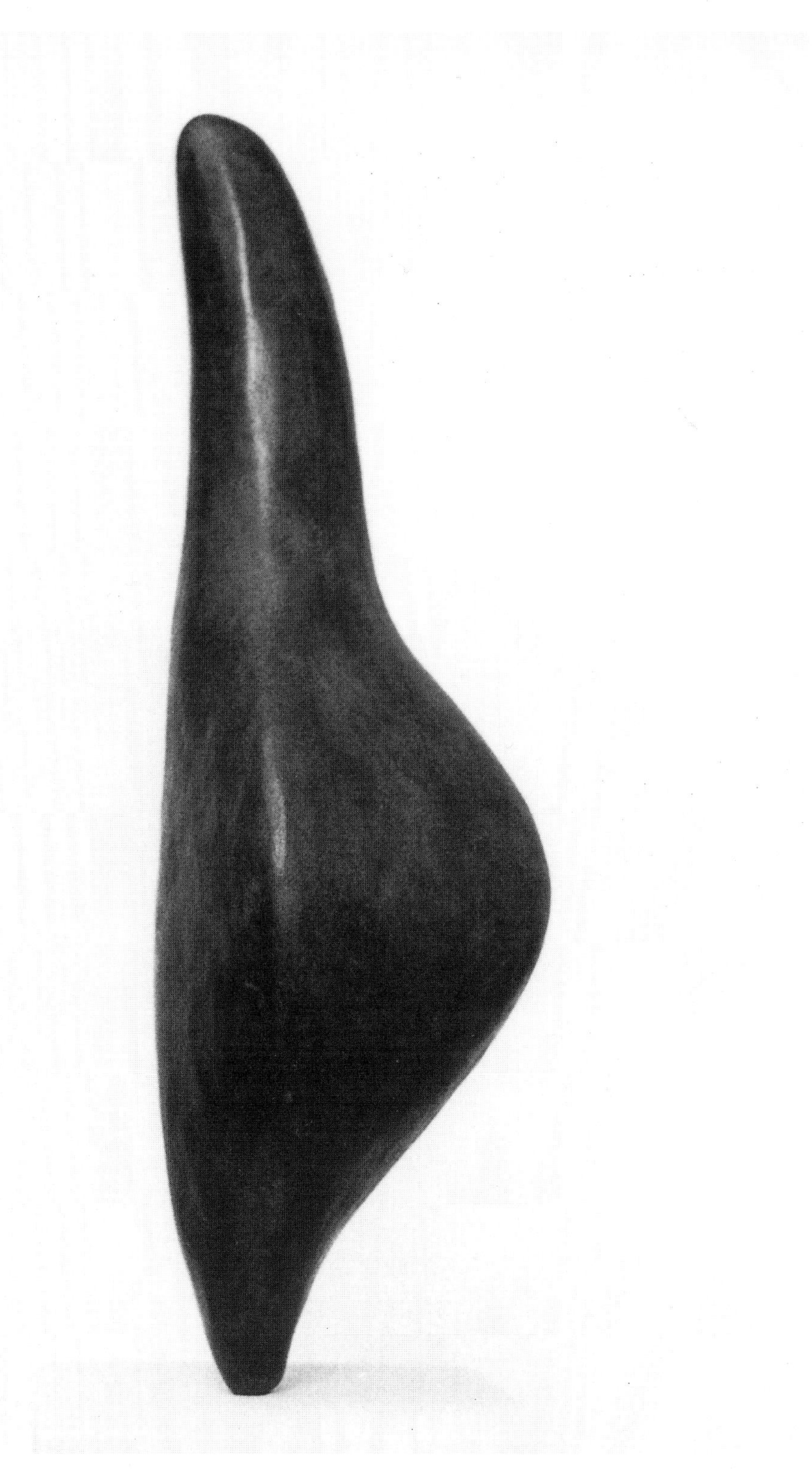

47 Leda 1982, bronze on stone base, bronze 24½ x 11¾ x 7⅜ in/
62.2 x 29.8 x 18.7 cm, base 11 x 8 x 3 in/28 x 20.3 x 7.6 cm. Edition of 6. The artist, courtesy Waddington Galleries

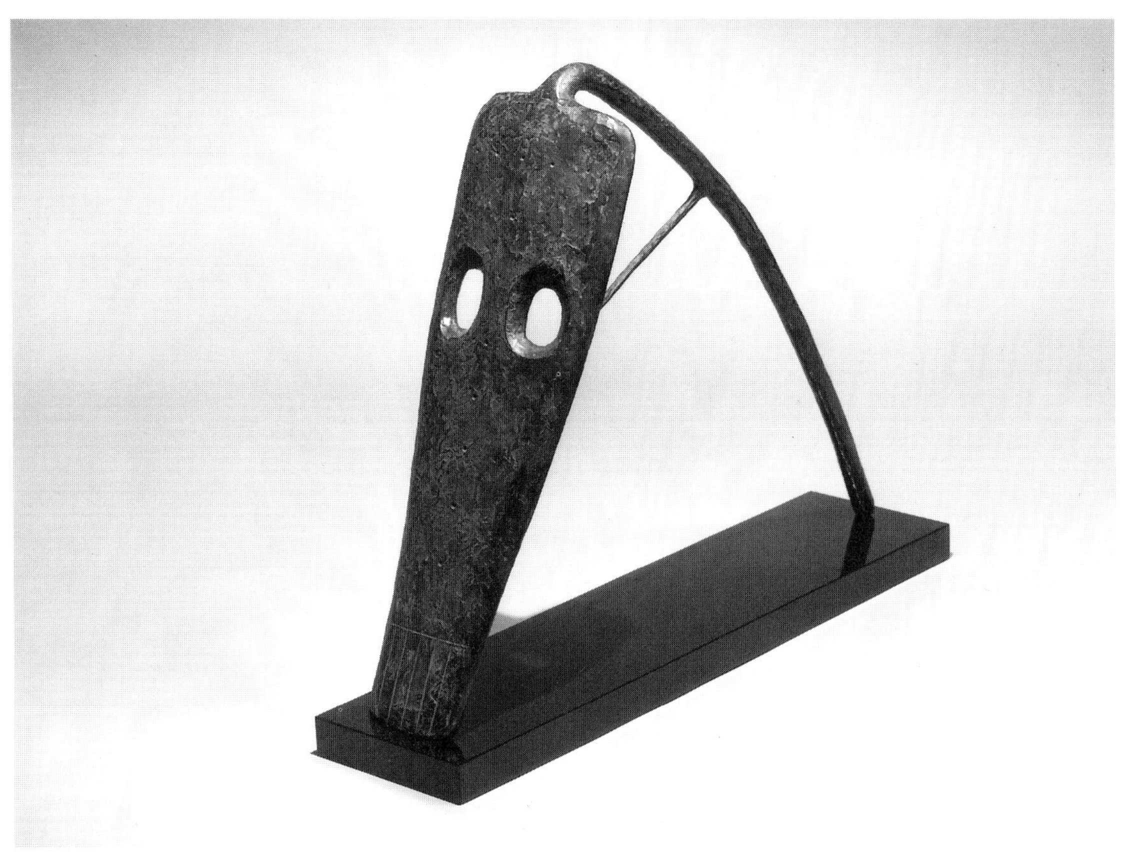

conscious of the consistency in his work, made him feel that it would be rewarding to return to an 'innocent' state, to make sculpture as if he had never made any before. The exhibition did, also, occur at a time when the artist felt he had taken the steel and related works to their logical conclusion. For some time he stopped making sculpture and concentrated exclusively on painting. Then, in the mid-1970s, he began to make small clay figures which he modelled by hand in a rough and ready way, trying, as he had in his work of the early 1950s, to avoid making conscious decisions. Using a type of clay that remained hard and permanent once dry, he simply took small lumps of it, modelled it quickly with his fingers, and then stored the objects without a second thought. Over a period of two or three years he produced hundreds of these works, most of them about the size of the palm of the hand.

From 1977–78 he began sorting through these clay studies, casting some directly in bronze

▷

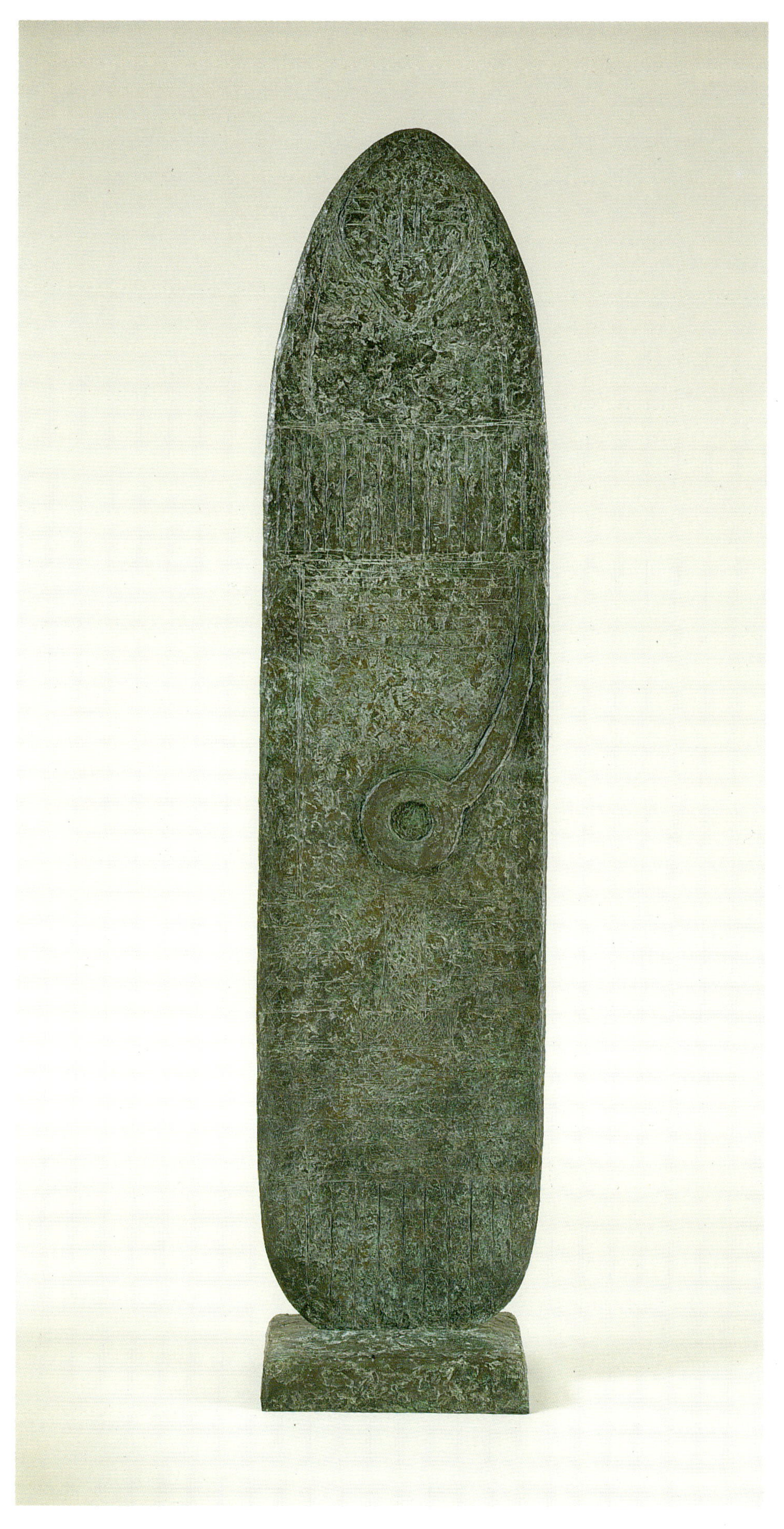

49 Ancestral Figure 1988
bronze, 82½ x 18¾ x 10¾ in/209.6 x 47.6 x 27.3 cm. Edition of 6. The artist, courtesy Waddington Galleries

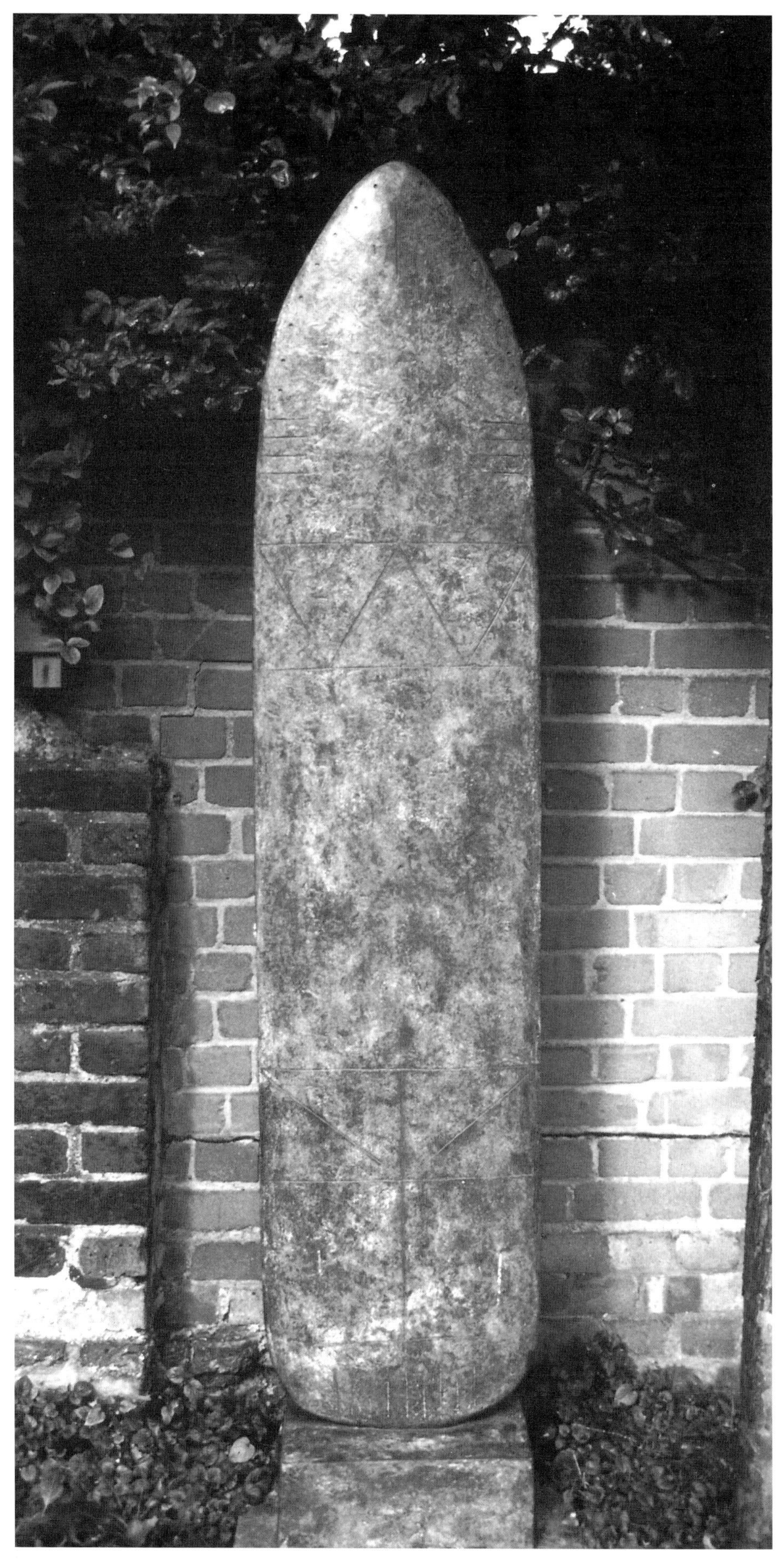

50 Queen 1 1987
bronze, 75¾ x 16 x 9¼ in/192.4 x 40.6 x 23.5 cm. Edition of 4 plus 1 artist's copy. The artist, courtesy Waddington Galleries

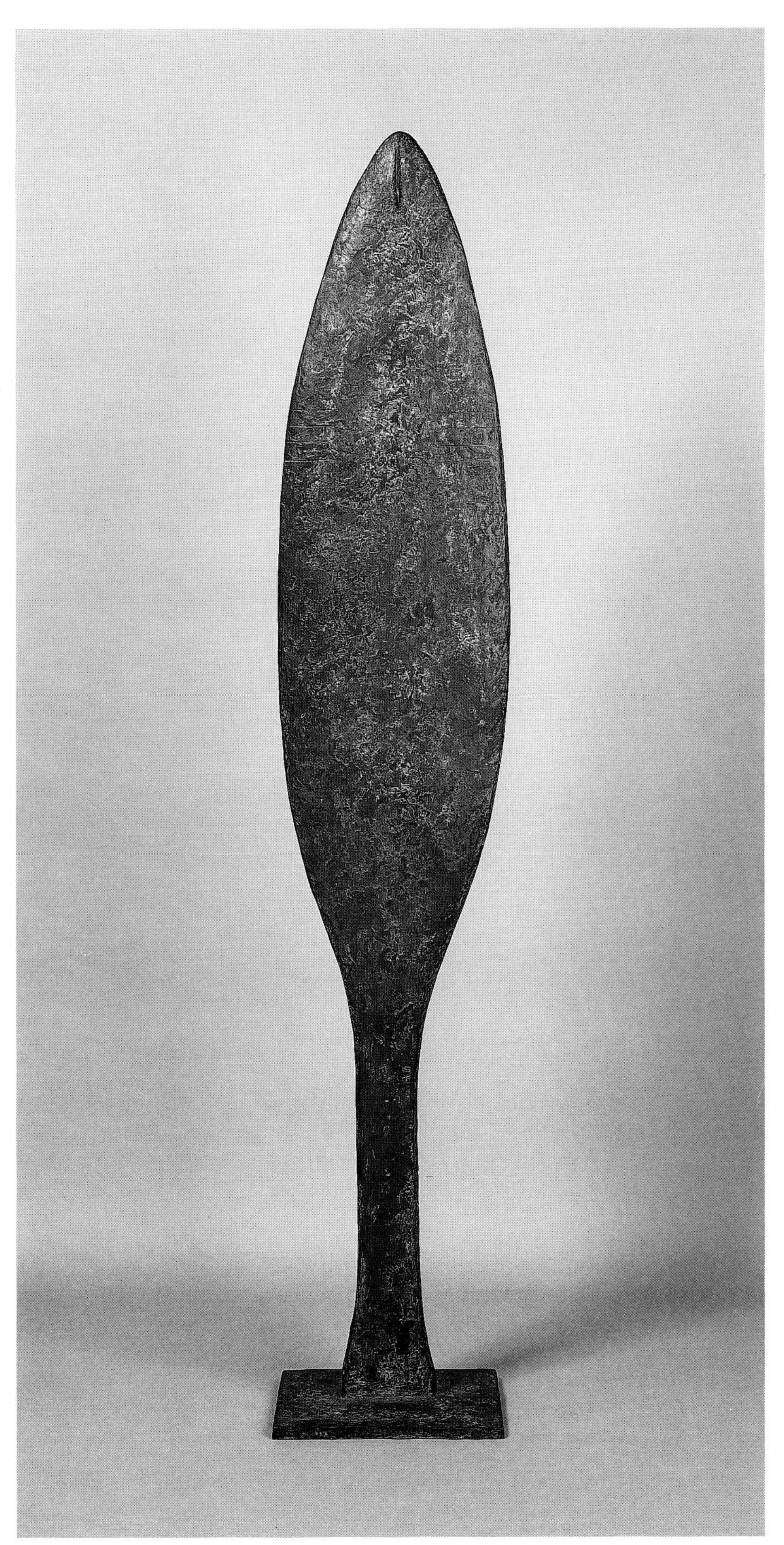

51 Paddle Venus 2 1986
bronze, 77½ x 13½ x 11¾ in/196.9 x 34.3 x 29.8 cm, Edition of 4 plus 1 artist's copy. The artist, courtesy Waddington Galleries

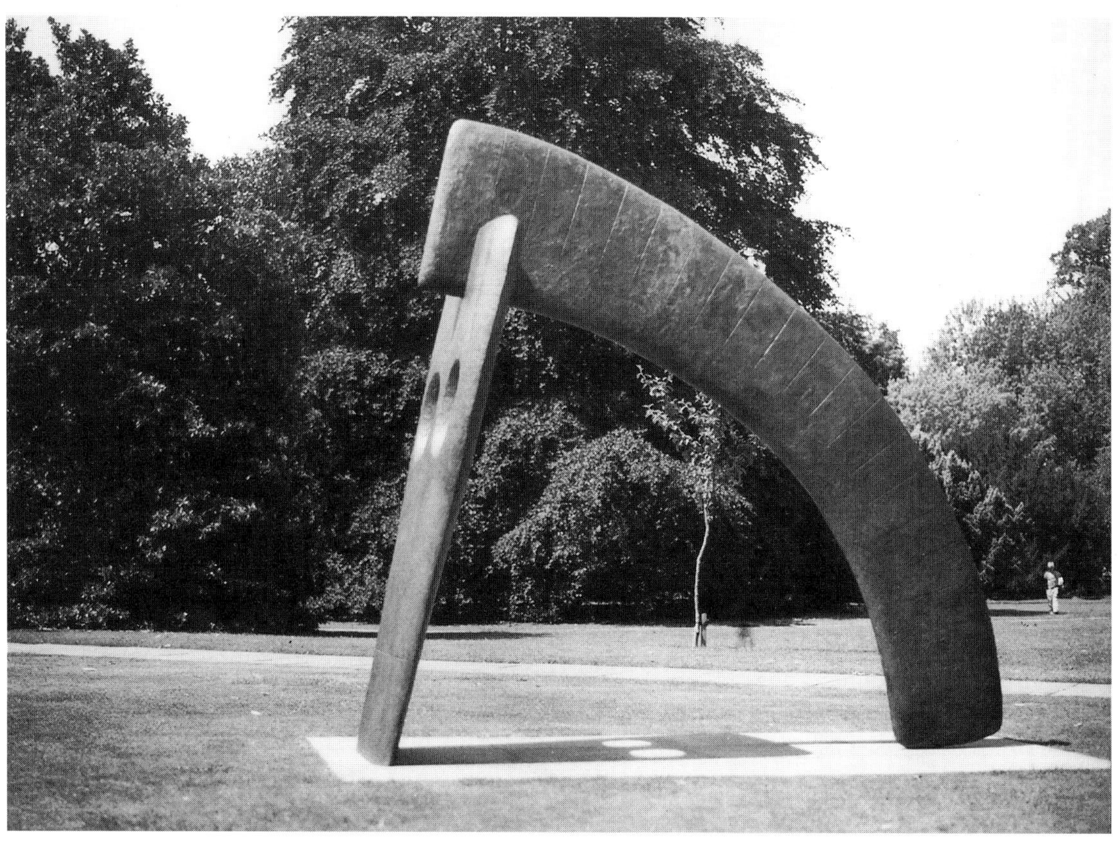

and developing others into slightly larger forms. The works of this period have a very primitive aspect, resembling arrow-heads and axe-heads (*Axe-head torso*, 1979) or ancient *Venus* figures which had been pulled out of the ground in a battered, limbless state. Often they are a strange combination of tool shape and torso shape, in the way that fragments of Cycladic art can often be. These works were shown at the Waddington Galleries, London, in 1981.

In the 1980s Turnbull began to work in a larger scale, for example in *Large Metamorphic Venus* of 1983 and in a series of *Paddle Venus* sculptures begun in 1985 (plate 51). These works relate to the bronzes of the 1950s, but they are at the same time the product of the steel works of the 1960s in their emphasis on clearly articulated, smooth, planar forms. Some of the works have particular sources. The *Paddle Venus* figures were inspired by 'bull-roarers' – flat, spear-shaped pieces of wood attached to lengths of string which witch-doctors would spin around their heads. Scarcely deviating from the shape of the wooden implement, Turnbull trans-

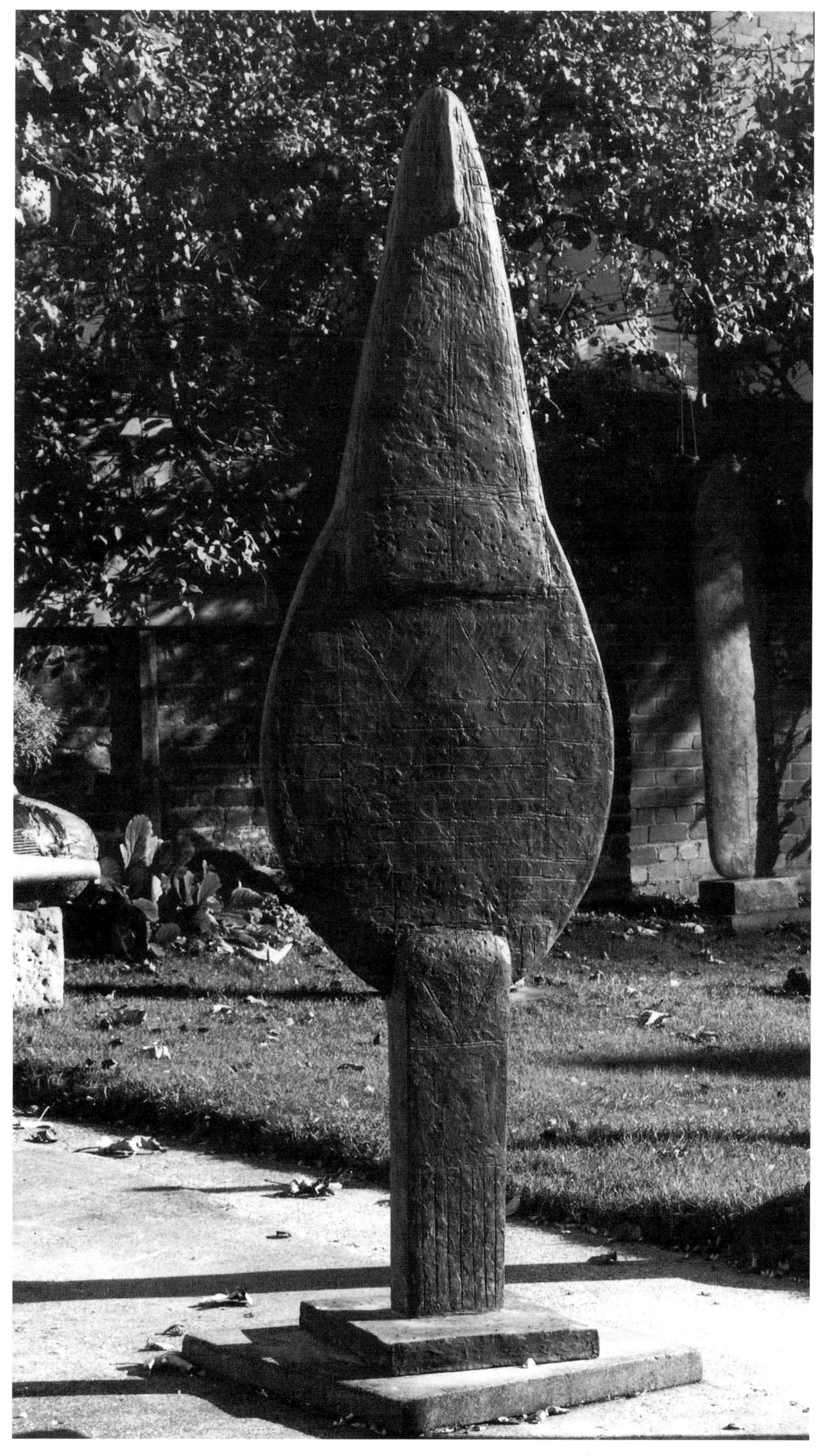

53 Idol 1988
bronze, 79½ x 23¾ x 15¾in/201.9 x 60.3 x 40cm. Edition of 4 plus 1 artist's copy. The artist, courtesy Waddington Galleries

formed it into a primitive idol. The series of *Horse* sculptures (*Horse 5*, 1988, and *Large Horse*, 1989–90), which are comparable to the *Horse* made at the Slade some forty years earlier, have their origin in the adzes Turnbull had seen in the East, the wooden handle metamorphosing into an elegant neck and the blade becoming a head. The *Sirens* of 1986 echo the form and colour of the giant, succulent leaves he had seen on his regular visits to Singapore, while the form of the *Blade Venus* series, the tallest of which is about ten foot in height (*Large Blade Venus*, 1990), originates in Japanese swords and Chinese chopping knives. Turnbull's art has always hinged on this process of metamorphosis, of a commonplace object such as a leaf, a knife or a grandfather clock magically changing into an archaic idol. A mundane object is just as likely to attract his eye as a museum object. The monumental *Queen* sculptures of 1987–88 (plates 50, 55), so majestic that one could imagine crowds of worshippers kneeling before them, have an unlikely source in his sons' surfboards and skateboards. Whereas in the 1960s Turnbull was making minimal alterations to rosewood logs and to steel bars, in the 1980s he was taking simple forms from the world around him and was introducing them into his sculpture. Through the addition of roughly scratched, iconic marks, the form would acquire a loosely figurative identity.

Turnbull's work displays a rare consistency. Though he has worked in a great variety of materials and with a number of different processes, from modelling to carving, welding to painting, he has always been preoccupied by certain fundamental concerns. Whatever the material and technique, the work is always characterized by simple, clearly articulated forms. It is not a stylistic quality that binds his work together, indeed one can hardly speak of his work as having a particular style. It is more to do with a consistent way of thinking, a way of thinking characterized by lucidity, decisiveness and economy of expression.

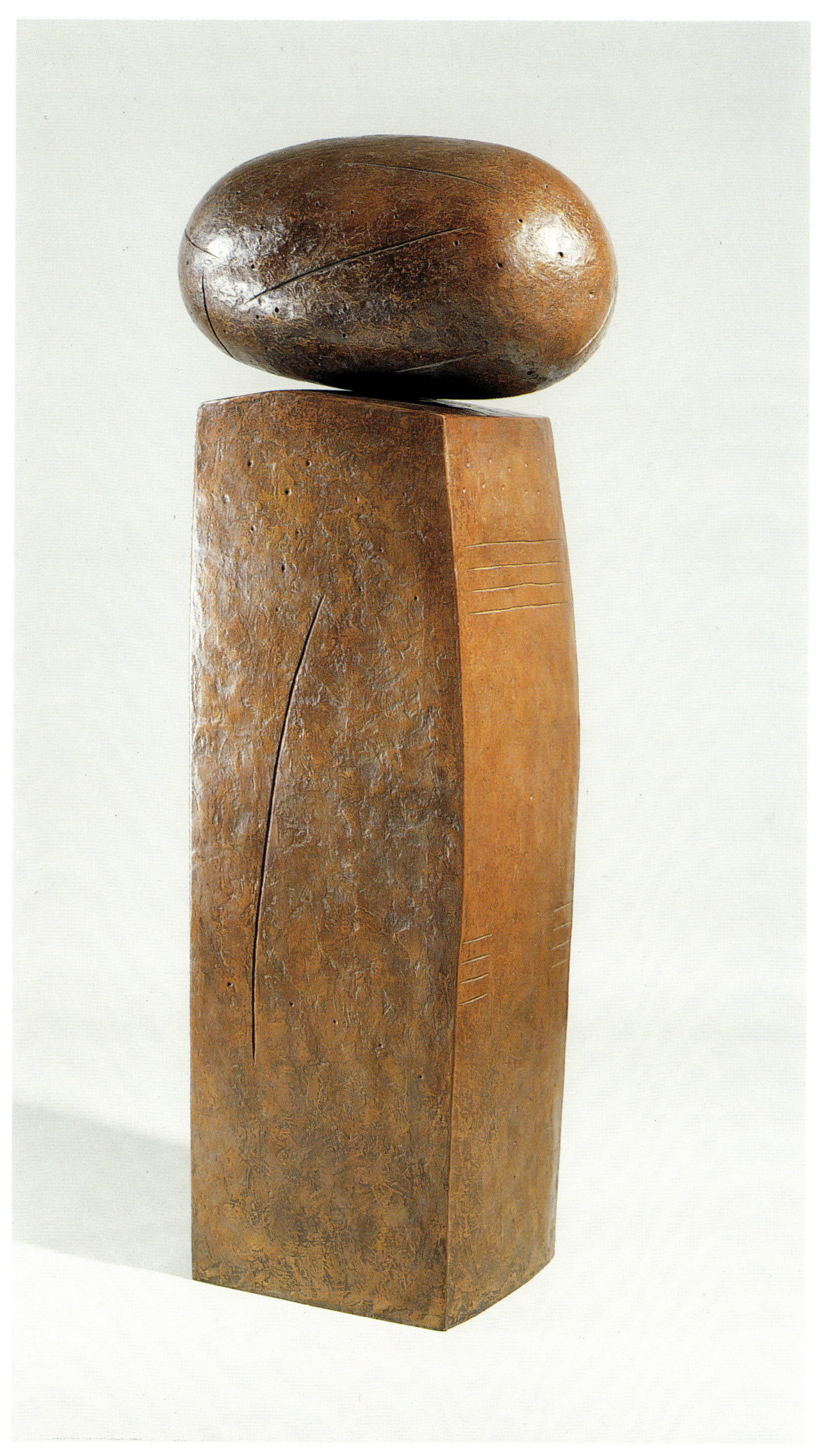

54 Male figure 1988
bronze, 72¾ x 15¾ x 29 in/184.8 x 40 x 73.7 cm. Edition of 6. The artist, courtesy Waddington Galleries

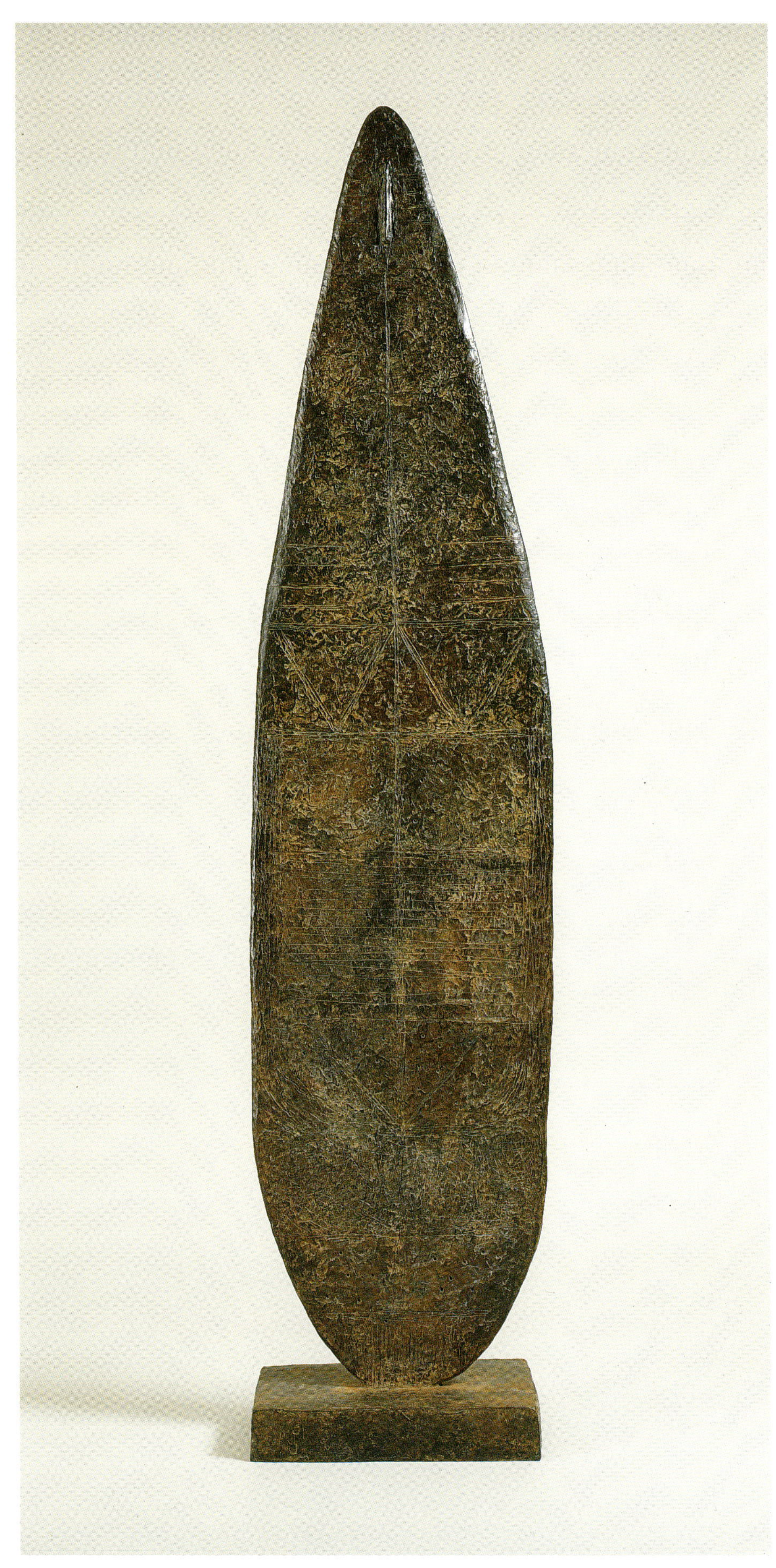

55 Queen 2 1988
bronze, 83½ x 19¼ x 11 in/212 x 48.9 x 27.9 cm. Edition of 4 plus 1 artist's copy. The artist, courtesy Waddington Galleries

Bronze Idols and Untitled Paintings, Serpentine Gallery, London, 15 November 1995 – 7 January 1996: Works in the Exhibition

Horse 1954 plate 7
Private collection, London

Head 2 1955 plate 8
Private collection, London

Metamorphosis 1955 plate 10
The artist, courtesy Waddington
Galleries

Drum 1956 plate 13
The artist, courtesy Waddington
Galleries

Totemic figure 1957 plate 15
Private collection, London

Aphrodite 1958 plate 19
The artist, courtesy Waddington
Galleries

5–1958 plate 23
The artist, courtesy Waddington
Galleries

7–1958 plate 25
The artist, courtesy Waddington
Galleries

15–1958 plate 21
Private collection, London

29–1958 plate 16
The artist, courtesy Waddington
Galleries

25–1959 plate 24
The artist, courtesy Waddington
Galleries

Lotus 1962 not illustrated
bronze, $12^{1}/_{2} \times 17$ in/31.8×43.2 cm
diameter
Private collection, London

Oedipus 2 1962 plate 28
Private collection, London

12–1963 plate 33
The artist, courtesy Waddington
Galleries

13–1968 plate 33
The artist, courtesy Waddington
Galleries

3–1976 plate 40
The artist, courtesy Waddington
Galleries

11–1976 plate 43
The artist, courtesy Waddington
Galleries

Leaf Venus 2 1986 plate 45
The artist, courtesy Waddington
Galleries

Paddle Venus 2 1986 plate 51
The artist, courtesy Waddington
Galleries

Horse 3 1987 plate 48
The artist, courtesy Waddington
Galleries

Queen 1 1987 plate 50
The artist, courtesy Waddington
Galleries

Queen 2 1988 plate 55
The artist, courtesy Waddington
Galleries

Idol 1988 plate 53
The artist, courtesy Waddington
Galleries

Ancestral figure 1988 plate 49
The artist, courtesy Waddington
Galleries

Blade Venus 1 1989 not illustrated
bronze on stone base, $43^{1}/_{2} \times 10^{3}/_{8} \times 5^{1}/_{2}$ in/$110.5 \times 26.4 \times 14$ cm
Edition of 6
The artist, courtesy Waddington
Galleries

Blade Venus 3 1989 plate 66
The artist, courtesy Waddington
Galleries

Blade Venus 4 1989 not illustrated
bronze on stone base, $73^{1}/_{4} \times 23 \times 10$ in/186×58.4 25.4 cm
Edition of 6
The artist, courtesy Waddington
Galleries

Large Blade Venus 1990 plate 68
The artist, courtesy Waddington
Galleries

Female 1990 plate 65
The artist, courtesy Waddington
Galleries

Mask 1 1991 plate 60
The artist, courtesy Waddington
Galleries

Head 2 1992 plate 61
The artist, courtesy Waddington
Galleries

Head 3 1992 not illustrated
bronze on stone base, bronze $13^{1}/_{2} \times 8^{1}/_{4} \times 5$ in/$34.2 \times 21 \times 12.7$ cm, base $2^{3}/_{4} \times 5^{1}/_{2} \times 5$ in/$7 \times 14 \times 12.7$ cm
Edition of 6
Private collection, London

Tall balance 1992 plate 64
The artist, courtesy Waddington
Galleries

Figure 1992 plate 63
The artist, courtesy Waddington
Galleries

1–1993 plate 56
The artist, courtesy Waddington
Galleries

2–1993 plate 57
The artist, courtesy Waddington
Galleries

5–1994 plate 59
The artist, courtesy Waddington
Galleries

6–1994 plate 58
The artist, courtesy Waddington
Galleries

Horse's head 1994 plate 67
The artist, courtesy Waddington
Galleries

56   1–1993
oil on canvas, 60 x 40 in/152.4 x 101.6 cm. The artist, courtesy Waddington Galleries

57   2–1993
oil on canvas, 60 x 40 in/152.4 x 101.6 cm. The artist, courtesy Waddington Galleries

58 6–1994
oil on canvas, 60 x 45 in/152.4 x 114.3 cm. The artist, courtesy Waddington Galleries

59 5-1994
oil on canvas, 60 x 40 in/152.4 x 101.6 cm. The artist, courtesy Waddington Galleries

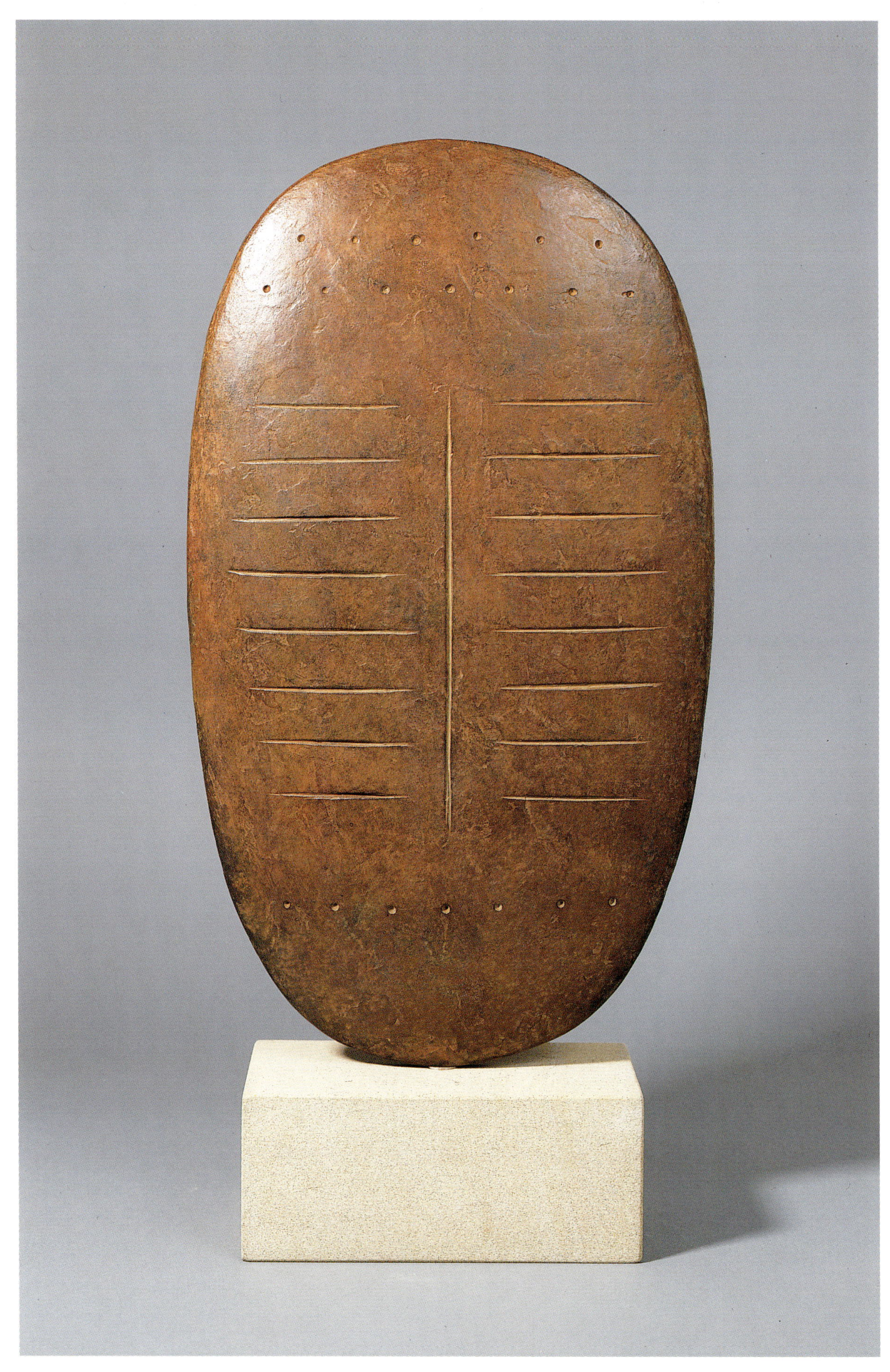

60 Mask 1 1991
bronze on stone base, bronze 17⅝ x 10 x 1⅝ in/44.7 x 25.4 x 4 cm. Edition of 6. The artist, courtesy Waddington Galleries

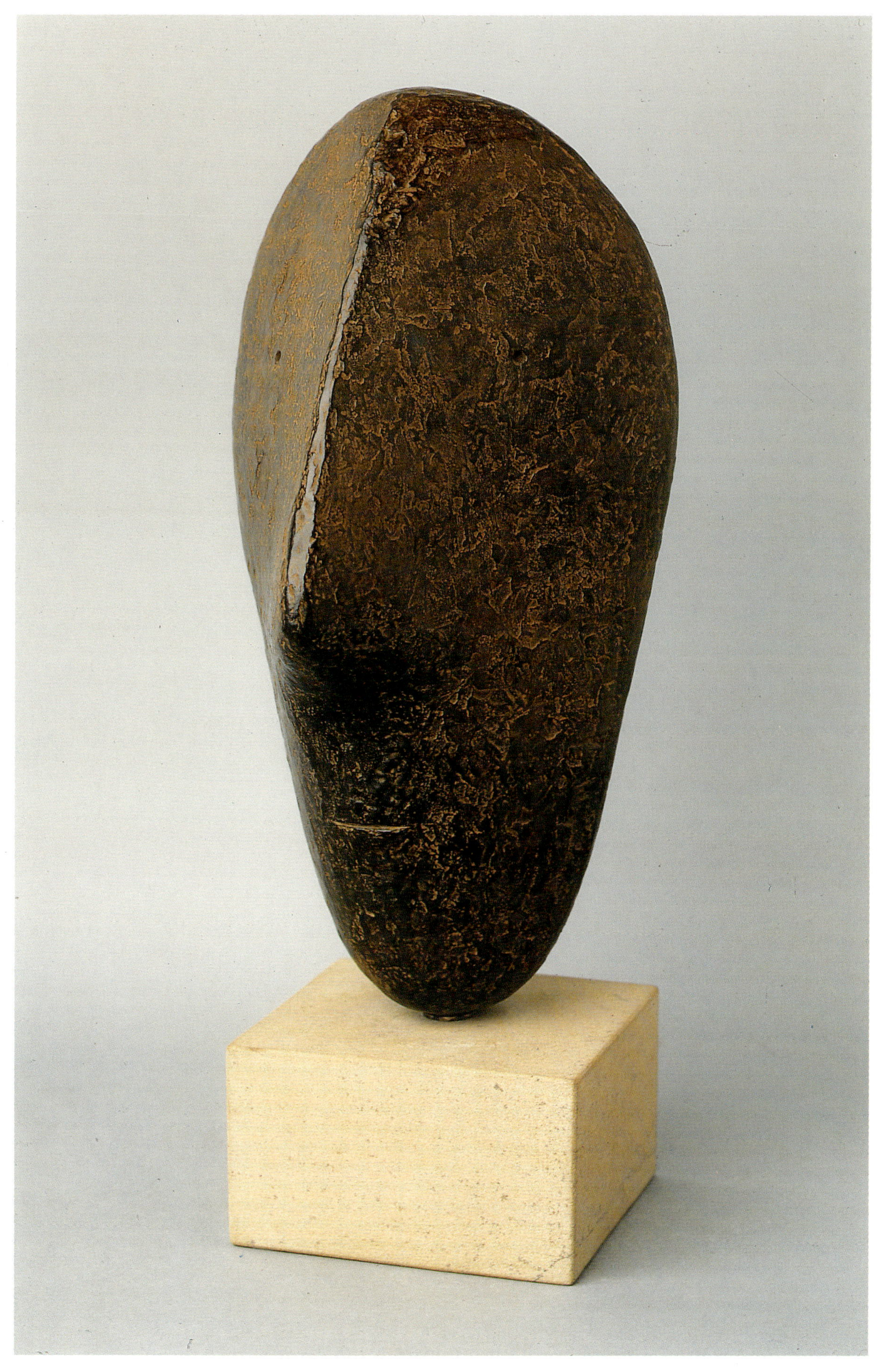

61 Head 2 1992, bronze on stone base, bronze 12¾ x 6½ x 7 in/
32.4 x 16.5 x 17.8 cm, base 2¾ x 5 x 4½ in/7 x 12.7 x 11.4 cm. Edition of 6. The artist, courtesy Waddington Galleries

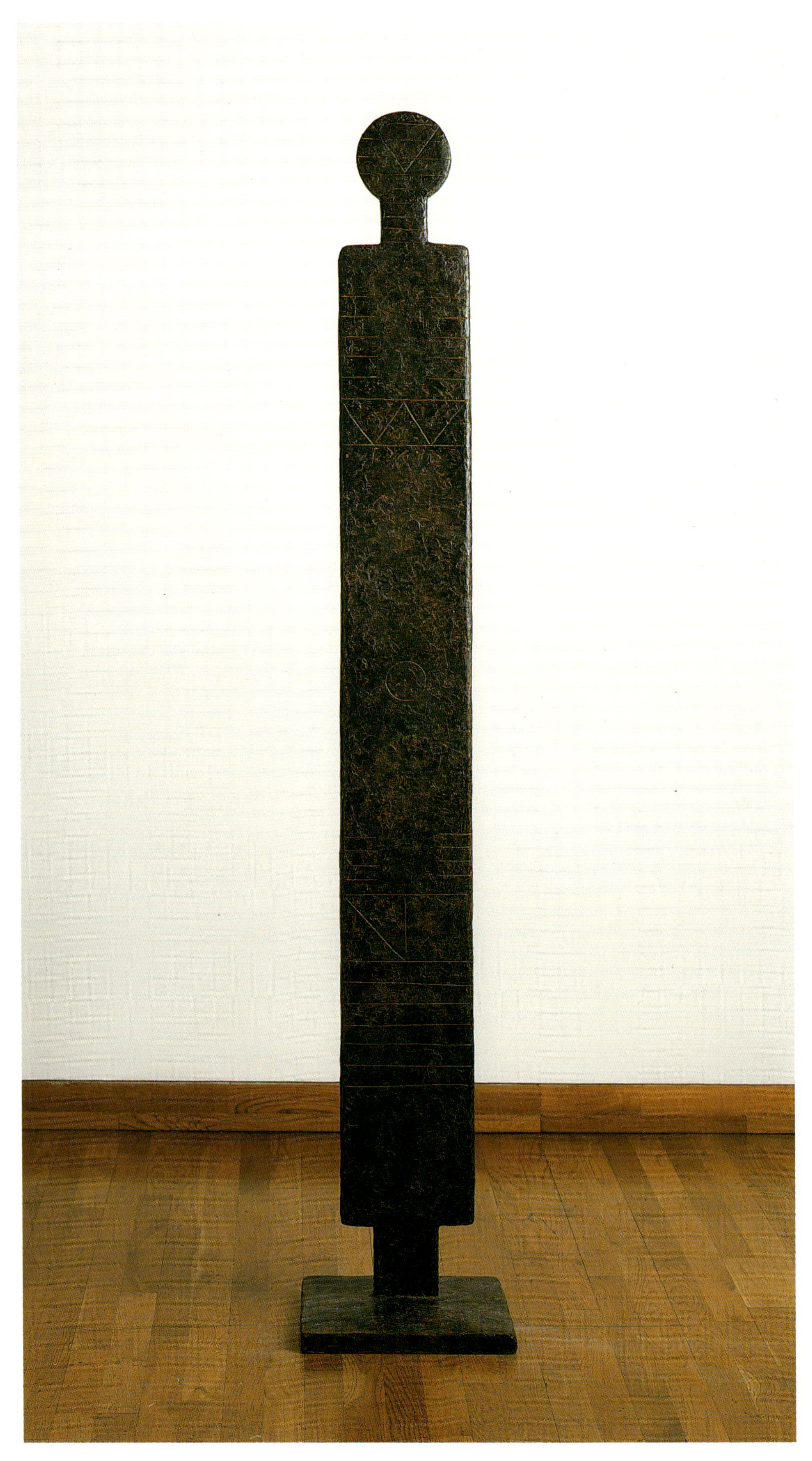

62 Female figure 1990
bronze, 82 x 14¼ x 12¾ in/208.3 x 36.2 x 32.4 cm. Edition of 6. The artist, courtesy Waddington Galleries

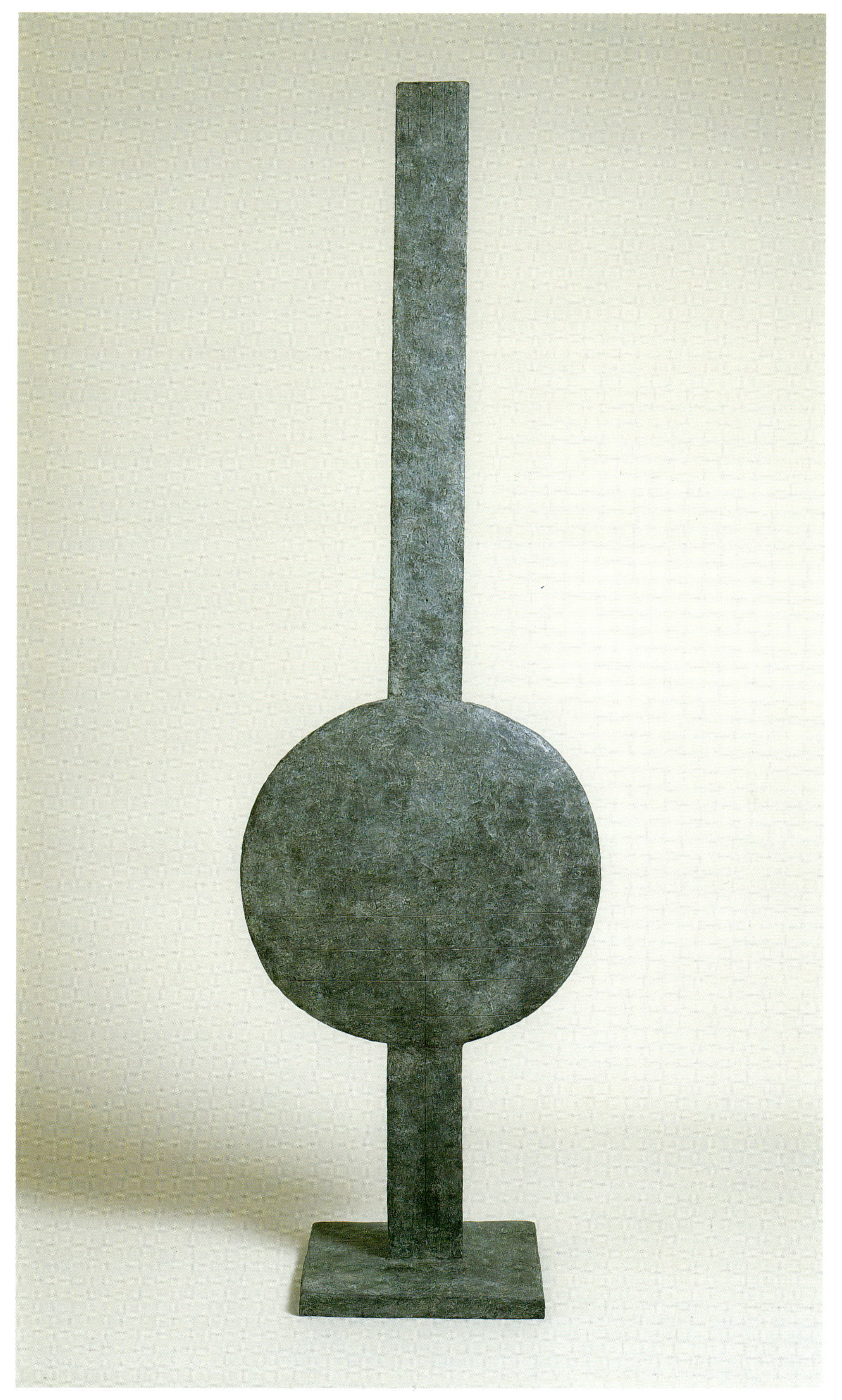

63 Figure 1992
bronze, 86¼ x 26 x 16¾ in/219 x 66 x 42.5 cm. Edition of 6. The artist, courtesy Waddington Galleries

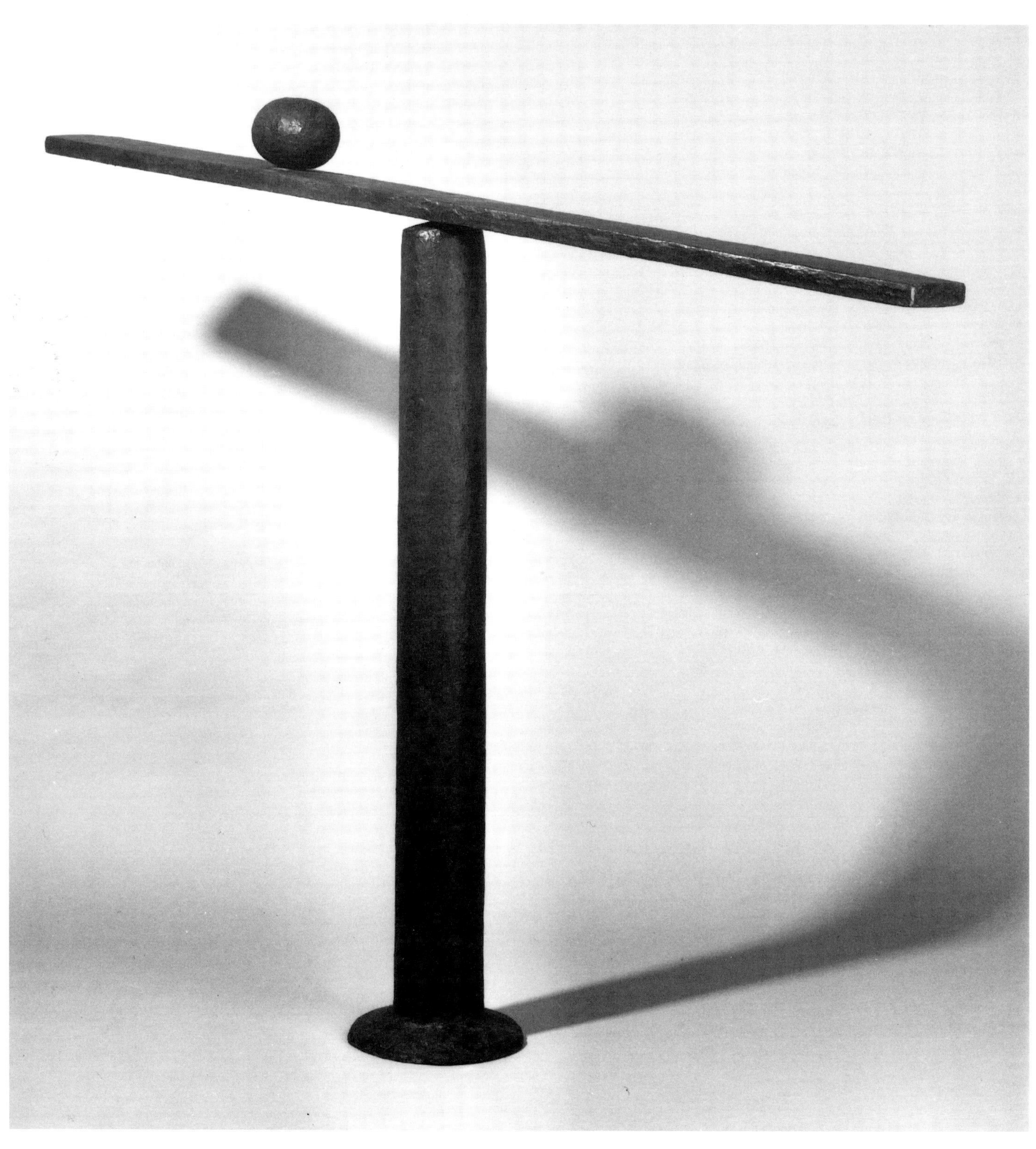

64 Tall balance 1992
bronze, 61¼ x 71 x 11 in/155.6 x 180.4 x 28 cm. Edition of 6. The artist, courtesy Waddington Galleries

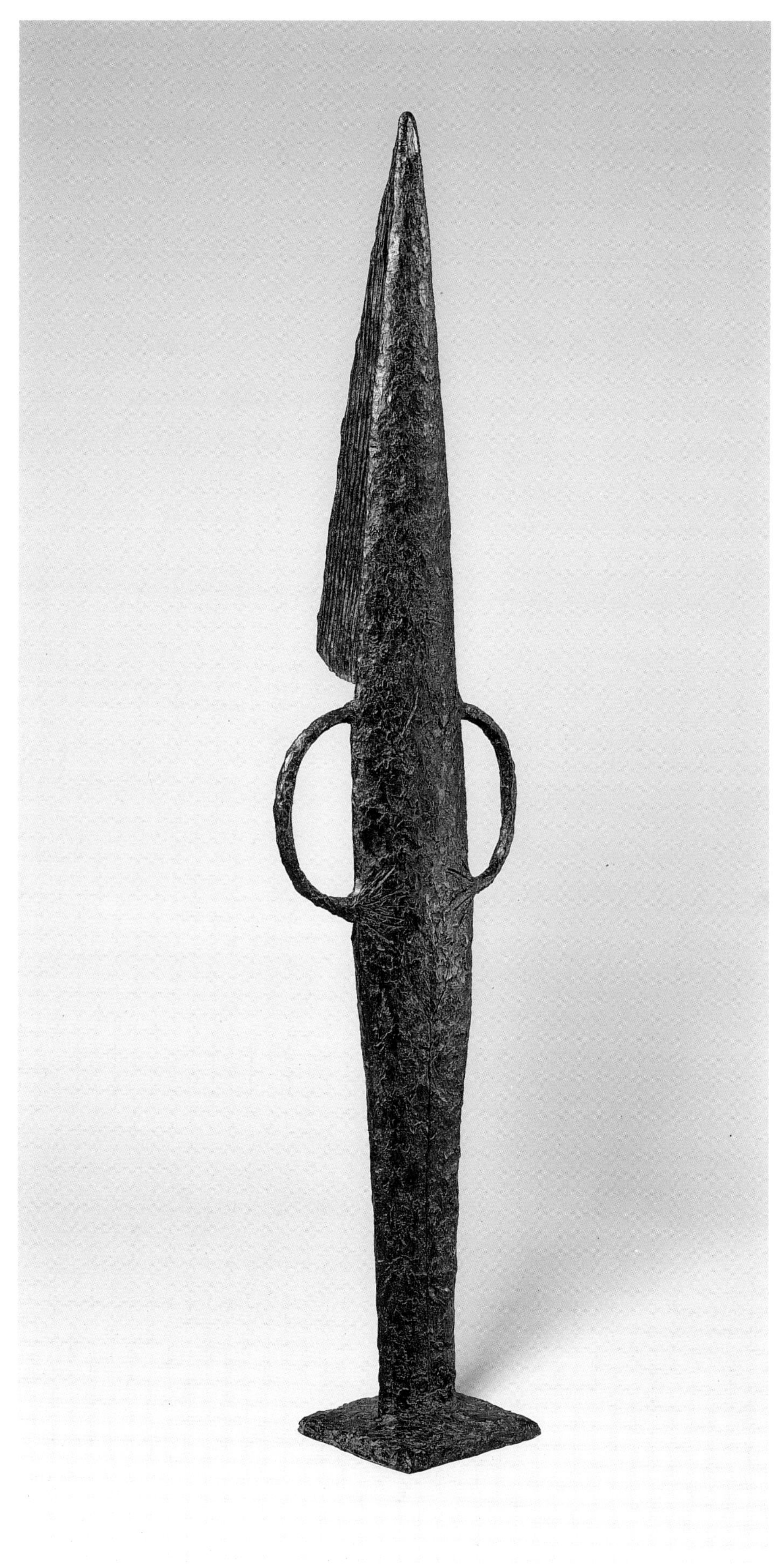

65 Female 1990
bronze, 66½ x 16½ x 12½ in / 168.9 x 41.9 x 31.7 cm, Edition of 6. The artist, courtesy Waddington Galleries

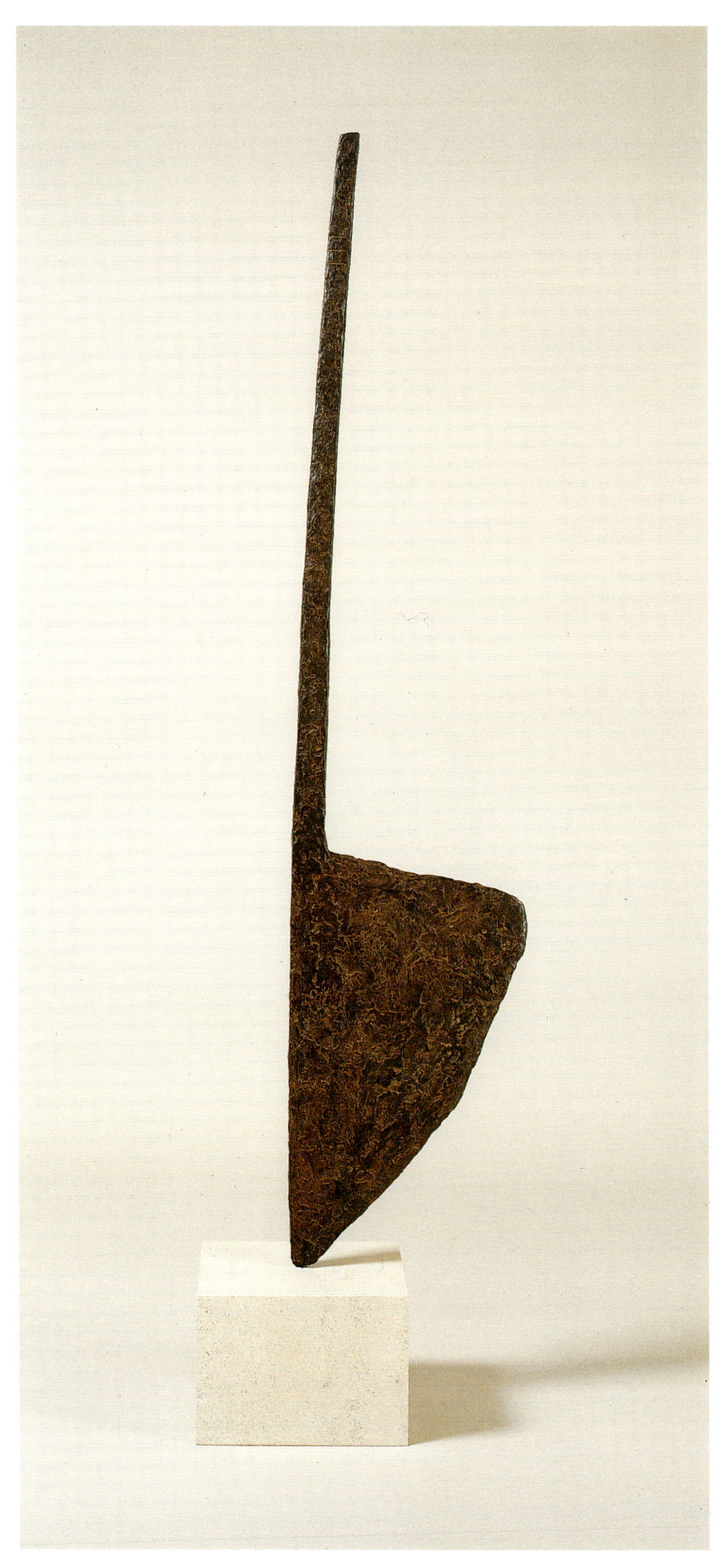

66 Blade Venus 3 1989, bronze on stone base, bronze 55½ x 11⅝ x 1¼ in/
141 x 29.5 x 3.2 cm, base 7 x 10 x 10 in/17.8 x 25.4 x 25.4 cm. Edition of 6. The artist, courtesy Waddington Galleries

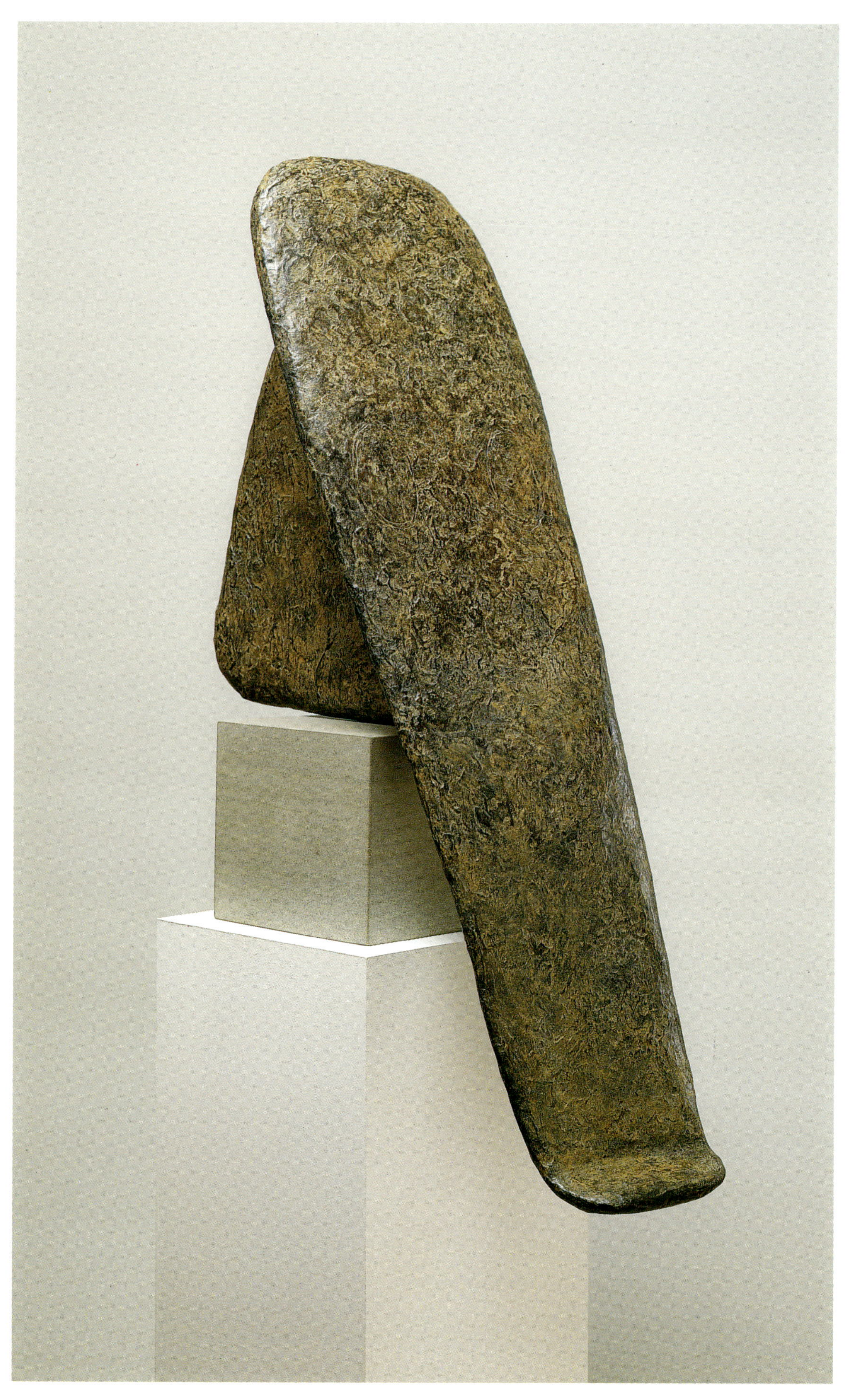

67 Horse's Head 1994, bronze on stone base, bronze 31⅞ x 9½ x 22⅜ in/
80.8 x 24 x 56.9 cm, base 6⅜ x 7⅜ x 7⅜/16.3 x 18.8 x 18.8 cm. Edition of 6. The artist, courtesy Waddington Galleries

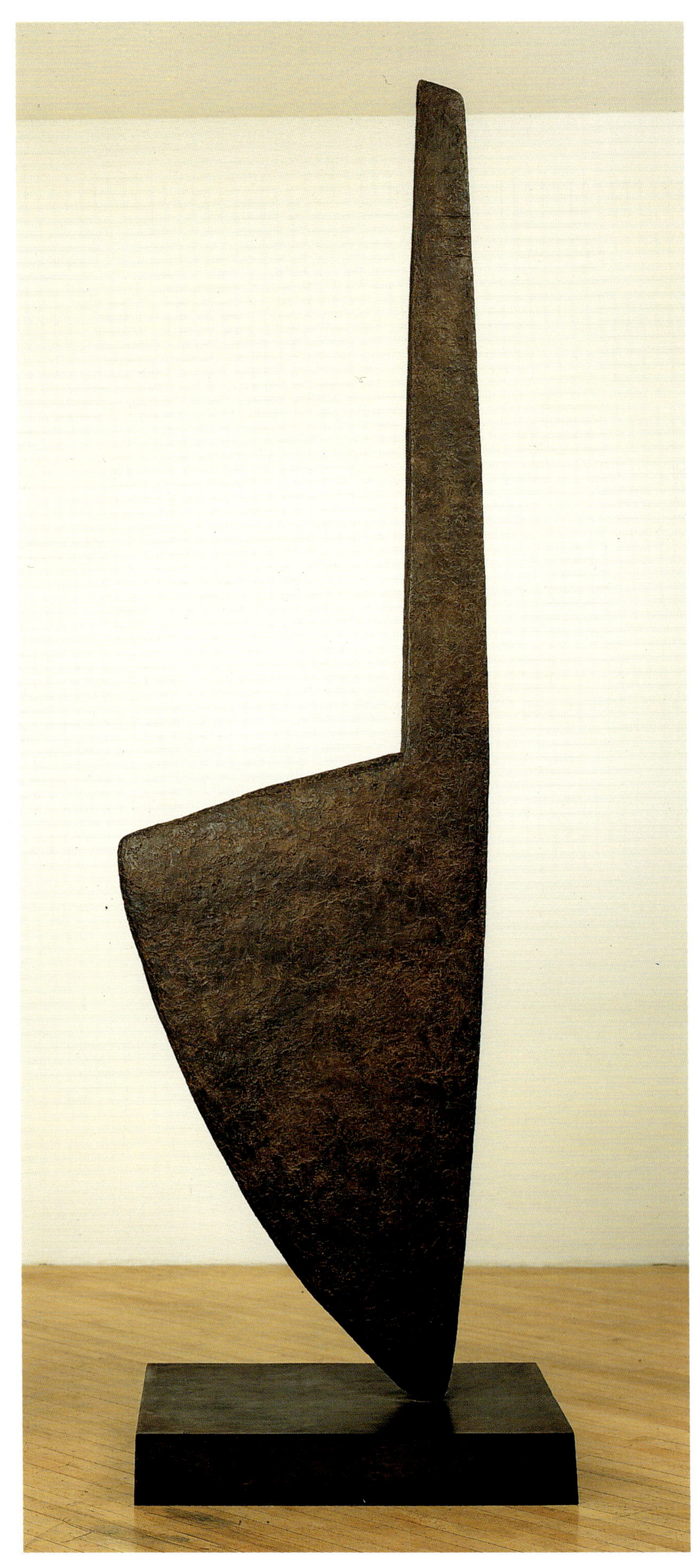

68 Large Blade Venus 1990
bronze, 125 x 39 x 26¾ in/317.5 x 99.1 x 68 cm. Edition of 5. The artist, courtesy Waddington Galleries

Appendix

BIOGRAPHY

1922 Born Dundee, Scotland, 11 January

1939–41 Worked in illustration department of a national periodical company, Dundee

1946–48 Studied at Slade School of Fine Art, London

1948–50 Lived in Paris

1950 Took up permanent residence in London

First solo exhibition, Hanover Gallery, London

1952–61 Visiting Artist, taught at the Central School of Arts and Crafts, London

1957 First visit to USA

1960 Married sculptor and printmaker, Kim Lim: two sons

1962 First travels in Japan, Cambodia, Malaysia

1964–72 Taught sculpture at the Central School of Arts and Crafts, London

Lives and works in London

ARTIST'S STATEMENTS

1956 'This is Tomorrow' (catalogue), Whitechapel Art Gallery, London

1960 'William Turnbull: Painter Sculptor', Uppercase 4

1961 'The Joining Edge', Gazette, No.1

1963 'Images without Temples', (statement and photographs), Living Arts, no.1, pp.14–27

1968 'Notes on Sculpture', Studio International, vol.176, November, pp.198–201

1969 'Colour in Sculpture', Studio International, vol.177, January, p.24

1972 'Liverpool', Studio International, July/August

SOLO EXHIBITIONS

1950 Hanover Gallery, London (sculpture)

1952 Hanover Gallery, London (sculpture and paintings)

1957 Institute of Contemporary Arts, London (sculpture and paintings)

1960 Molton Gallery, London (sculpture)

1961 Molton Gallery, London (paintings)

1963 Marlborough-Gerson Gallery, New York (sculpture)

Art Institute, Detroit (sculpture)

1965 Bennington College, Vermont (paintings)

Galerie Muller, Stuttgart (paintings)

1966 Pavilion Gallery, Balboa, California (sculpure and paintings)

1967 Waddington Galleries, London (sculpture and paintings)

1967–68 IX Bienal, Saõ Paolo; touring to Museo de Arte Moderna, Rio de Janeiro; Museo National de Belles Artes, Buenos Aires; Institute de Artes Plasticas, Santiago (sculpture and paintings)

1968 Hayward Gallery, London (paintings)

1969 Waddington Galleries, London (lithographs)

1970 Waddington Galleries, London (sculpture and paintings)

1973 Tate Gallery, London (sculpture and paintings retrospective)

1974 Scottish Arts Council, Edinburgh (sculpture, paintings and prints)

Galerie Muller, Stuttgart (paintings)

1976 Waddington Galleries, London (paintings and prints)

1978 Waddington and Tooth Galleries, London (drawings)

1981 Waddington Galleries, London (sculpture)

The Scottish Gallery, Edinburgh (sculpture)

1982 Waddington Galleries, Toronto and New York (sculpture)

1983 Galerie Kutter, Luxembourg (sculpture)

1984 National Museum Art Gallery, Singapore (sculpture, with Kim Lim)

1985 Waddington Galleries, London (sculpture)

1986 Terry Dintenfass Inc., New York (sculpture)

1987 Galerie Folker Skulima, Berlin (sculpture)

Waddington Galleries, London (sculpture retrospective)

1988 Terry Dintenfass Inc., New York (sculpture)

1988–89 John Berggruen Gallery, San Francisco (sculpture)

1989 Arnold Herstand Gallery, New York (sculpture and drawings)

1990 'Sculpture in the Close', Jesus College, Cambridge

1991 Waddington Galleries, London (sculpture)/The Economist Plaza, St James's, London (sculpture)

1992 Galeria Freites, Caracas (sculpture)

Galerie Michael Haas, Berlin (sculpture)

Galerie von Braunbehrens, Munich (sculpture)

1994 Galerie Sander, Darmstadt (sculpture)

1995 Serpentine Gallery, London

SELECTED GROUP
EXHIBITIONS

1950 'Les mains éblouis', Galerie
Maeght, Paris

'Aspects of British Art', Institute of
Contemporary Arts, London

1951 'Abstract Art', Riverside
Museum, New York

1952 'Venice Biennale', British
Pavilion, Venice

'Young Sculptors', Institute of
Contemporary Arts, London

1956 'Contemporary Sculpture',
Hanover Gallery, London

1956–57 'Yngre Brittiska
Skulptorer', Gothenburg Museum;
touring to Sandviken; Linkoping;
Tranas; Lund; Halsingborg;
Halmstad; Falkenberg; Orebro;
Stockholm

1957 'Dimensions', O'Hana
Gallery, London

'Ten British Sculptors Exhibition',
Biennale Sao Paolo; touring to Rio
de Janeiro; Buenos Aires;
Montevideo; Santiago; Lima;
Caracas

1958 'Contemporary British
Sculpture', Arts Council of Great
Britain, London; touring to Japson
Gardens, Leamington Spa;
Shrewsbury Castle; Bute Park,
Cardiff

'Exploration of Form', Tooth
Gallery, London

'New Trends in British Art', New
York-Rome Art Foundation, Rome

'Pittsburgh International', Carnegie
Institute, Pittsburgh, Pennsylvania

1959 'Biennale', Middleheim,
Antwerp

'Bronzetti', Biennale d'Arte
Triveneta, Padua

1959–60 'European Art Today: 35
Painters and Sculptors', Minneapolis
Institute of Arts; touring to Los
Angeles County Museum; San
Francisco Museum of Art; North
Carolina Museum of Art; National
Gallery of Canada, Ottawa; French
& Co., New York; Baltimore
Museum of Art

1960 'Situation', R.B.A. Galleries,
London

1960 (cont.)

'The Mysterious Sign', Institute of
Contemporary Arts, London

'Sculpture in the Open Air',
Battersea Park, London

1961 'Bronzetti', Biennale d'Arte
Triveneta, Padua

'Ten Sculptors', Marlborough New
London Gallery

'New London Situation',
Marlborough New London Gallery

'2nd International Exhibition of
Sculpture', Musée Rodin, Paris

'Neue Malerei in England',
Stadtisches Museum, Leverkusen

'Pittsburgh International', Carnegie
Institute, Pittsburgh, Pennsylvania

1962 'Maestri de XIX/XX Secolo',
Marlborough Galleria d'Arte, Rome

'Aspects of 20th Century Art',
Marlborough Fine Art, London

'Hoyland, Plumb, Stroud, Turnbull',
Marlborough New London Gallery

'Premio International de
Escuoltura', Instituto di Tella,
Buenos Aires

'Mostra Internazionale de Scultura',
Galleria Toninelli, Spoleto

'Hirshhorn Collection', Solomon R.
Guggenheim Museum, New York

'British Art Today', San Francisco
Museum of Art; touring to Dallas
Museum of Contemporary Art;
Santa Barbara Museum of Art

'Pittsburgh International', Carnegie
Institute, Pittsburgh, Pennsylvania

1963 'Junge Englische Maler',
Kunsthalle, Basel

'7th International Art Exhibition',
Tokyo

'Sculpture in the Open Air',
Battersea Park, London

'IV Biennale Internazionale d'Arte',
San Marino, Italy

1964 'Contemporary British
Painting and Sculpture', Albright-
Knox Art Gallery, Buffalo, NY

'International Graphics', Albright-
Knox Art Gallery, Buffalo, NY

'Profile III, Englische Kunst der
Gegenwart', Städtisches
Kunstmuseum Bochum, Germany

1964 (cont.)

'Guggenheim International',
Solomon R. Guggenheim Museum,
New York

'Painting and Sculpture of a
Decade', Tate Gallery, London

1965 'British Sculpture in the
Sixties', Tate Gallery, London

'Signale', Kunsthalle, Basel

'Drawings from the Betty Parsons
Collection', New York

'Sculpture from the Albert A. List
Family Collection', New School Art
Center, New York

1966 'Sculpture in the Open Air',
Battersea Park, London

'Sonsbeek Park', Arnhem

'New Shapes and Forms of Colour',
Stedelijk Museum, Amsterdam

1967 'Formen der Farbe',
Württembergischer Kunstverein,
Stuttgart; touring to Kunsthalle,
Bern

'Guggenheim International',
Solomon R. Guggenheim Museum,
New York

1968 'Documenta 4', Kassel

'Sculpture in the City', Arts Council
Gallery, London; touring to Post &
Mail Building, Birmingham; Goree
Piazza, Liverpool; Southampton
Civic Centre

1969 'Middleheim Biennale',
Antwerp

'First International Exhibition of
Modern Sculpture', Hakone Open
Air Museum, Japan

1971 'McAlpine Collection', Tate
Gallery, London

1972 '20th Century Sculpture in
Los Angeles Collections', U.C.L.A.
Galleries, Los Angeles

1974 'Künstler machen Fahnen für
Rottweil', Stadtfest Rottweil,
Germany

'British Painting', Hayward Gallery,
London

'Artistas Graficos Britanicos de la
Decade del 60', British Council
exhibition; touring to Rio de
Janeiro, Recife, Belo Horizonte,
Brazilia, Sao Paolo, Curitiba, Porto
Alegre, Mar del Plata, Rosario,
Cordoba, Buenos Aires, Lima,
Bogota, Medelin, Cali, Barranquila

1975 'The Need to Draw', Scottish Arts Council Gallery, Edinburgh; touring to Aberdeen Art Gallery; Dundee City Art Gallery

1976 'Arte Inglese Oggi', Palazzo Reale, Milan

'The Human Clay', Hayward Gallery, London

1977 'Hayward Annual', Hayward Gallery, London

'Silver Jubilee Exhibition of British Sculpture', Battersea Park, London

'Color en la Pintura Britanica', British Council exhibition; touring to Rio de Janeiro, Brazilia, Curitiba, Sao Paolo, Buenos Aires, Caracas, Bogota, Mexico City

'Drawings and Watercolours of Distinction', Victor Waddington Gallery, London

'Private Images' (Photographs by Sculptors), Los Angeles County Museum of Art

'British Painting 1952–77', Royal Academy of Arts, London

1977–78 'Series', Tate Gallery, London

'Carved-Modelled-Constructed', Tate Gallery, London

1978 'Groups', Waddington & Tooth Galleries, London

'The Mechanised Image', Arts Council of Great Britain exhibition; touring to Portsmouth; Sheffield; London; Kingston-upon-Hull; Newcastle-upon-Tyne; Aberdeen

'The Museum of Drawers', Cooper-Hewitt Museum, New York; touring to Kunsthaus, Zürich

'John Moores Exhibition', Walker Art Gallery, Liverpool (2nd prize)

1979 'Sculpture Européenne', Château Malou, Brussels

'Groups II', Waddington Galleries, London

'Tate 79' (Inaugural exhibition for the new extension), Tate Gallery, London

1980 'Groups III', Waddington Galleries, London

1981 'Sculpture for the Blind', Tate Gallery, London

'Artists in Camden', Camden Arts Centre, London

1982 'British Sculpture in the 20th century: Part 2, Symbol and Imagination 1951–1980', Whitechapel Art Gallery, London

'A Selection from the permanent collection of prints', Tate Gallery, London

'Sculpture', Waddington Galleries, London

1983–84 'Views and Horizons', Yorkshire Sculpture Park, Wakefield

'Drawing in Air, an Exhibition of Sculptors Drawings 1882–1982', Sunderland Arts Centre exhibition, Ceolfrith Gallery, Sunderland; touring to Glynn Vivian Art Gallery & Museum, Swansea; City Art Gallery and Henry Moore Study Centre, Leeds

1985 'Sculptors' Drawings', Scottish Arts Council Gallery, Edinburgh

'Hands', Anne Berthoud Gallery, London

'Twenty-Five Years', Annely Juda/Juda Rowan Gallery, London

'Malerei Plastik Objekt', Museum Morsbroich, Leverkusen, Germany

1986 'Forty Years of Modern Art 1945–1985', Tate Gallery, London

'British Sculpture 1950–1965', New Art Centre, London

'From Figuration to Abstraction', Annely Juda Fine Art, London

'Sculpture and Works in Relief', John Berggruen Gallery, San Francisco

'Trends in Geometric Abstract Art: The Riklis Collection of the McCrory Corporation', Tel Aviv Museum, Israel

1987 'British Art in the Twentieth Century: The Modern Movement', Royal Academy of Arts, London; touring to Staatsgalerie Stuttgart, Germany

'Ancient & Modern', McAlpine Gallery, Ashmolean Museum, Oxford

'Forty Years of British Sculpture', National Gallery and Alexander Soutzos Museum, Athens

1988 'Abstract Art From Sheffield's Collection', Mappin Art Gallery, Sheffield

1988 (cont.)

'Sculpture', Waddington Galleries, London

'Britannica: Trente Ans de Sculpture 1960–1988', Musée des Beaux Arts, Le Havre; touring to Musée de l'Evèche, Evreux; Ecole d'Architecture de Normandie, Rouen; Museum Van Hedendaagse Kunst, Antwerp (here re-titled 'British Sculpture 1960–1988'); Centre Régional d'Art Contemporain, Toulouse

'Glasgow Garden Festival', Glasgow

'Minimalistische Tendenzen Sammlung Sybil Albers', Stiftung für Konstruktive und Konkrete Kunst, Zürich

'Modern British Sculpture from the Collection', Tate Gallery, Liverpool

1988–89 'Sculpteurs Anglais du XXième Siècle', Artcurial, Paris

1989 'The London Opening', Scottish Gallery, London

'From Picasso to Abstraction', Annely Juda Fine Art, London

'Post War Sculpture', Arnold Herstand & Company, New York

'Scottish Art Since 1900', Scottish National Gallery of Modern Art, Edinburgh; touring to Barbican Art Gallery, London

'Aus der Sammlung Sybil Albers – Barrier', Stiftung für Konstruktive und Konkrete Kunst, Zürich

1989–90 'From Prism to Paintbox: Colour Theory and Practice in British Painting', Oriel Gallery, Clwyd; touring to Warrington Museum & Art Gallery; Cooper Art Gallery, Barnsley

1990 'Studies on Paper, Contemporary British Sculptors', Connaught Brown, London

'20th Century Scottish Drawings', Scottish Gallery, Edinburgh

'164th Annual Exhibition 1990', Royal Scottish Academy, Edinburgh (Invited Guest Artist)

'New Hanging', Tate Gallery, London

'Hands', Grob Gallery, London

'For the Collector: Important 20th Century Sculpture', Meredith Long & Company, Houston, Texas

1990–91 'The Independent Group: Postwar Britain and the Aesthetics of Plenty', Institute of Contemporary Arts, London; touring to Instituto Valenciano De Arte Moderno, Centro Julio Gonzalez, Valencia; Museum of Contemporary Art, Los Angeles; University Art Museum, University of California at Berkeley; Hood Museum of Art, Dartmouth College, Hanover, New Hampshire

1991 'British Art from 1930', Waddington Galleries, London

'Avant-Garde British Printmaking 1914–60', The British Museum, London

'New Displays 1991', Tate Gallery, London

'Virtue and Vision: Sculpture and Scotland 1540–1990', Royal Scottish Academy, Edinburgh

'Saved for Scotland', National Gallery of Scotland, Edinburgh

'Sculpture Garden at Roche Court', New Art Centre, Wiltshire

'Sculpture by the Spire/Salisbury Festival', Salisbury Cathedral Close and Courcoux & Courcoux Gallery, Salisbury

1992 '4 Sculpteurs Anglais: Armitage, Caro, Chadwick, Turnbull', Artcurial, Paris

'Ready, Steady, Go: Painting of the Sixties from the Arts Council Collection', Royal Festival Hall, South Bank Centre, London; touring Britain

'Sculpture', Waddington Galleries, London

'New Realities, Art in Western Europe 1945–68', Tate Gallery, Liverpool

'Le Cri et la Raison, L'espace de l'art concret', Château de Mouans, Sartoux, Cotes d'Azur

'New Beginnings: Postwar British Art from the collection of Ken Powell', Scottish National Gallery of Modern Art, Edinburgh; touring to Graves Art Gallery, Sheffield

1993 'A Sculptor's Landscape', New Art Centre, London

'Sculpture Garden at Roche Court', New Art Centre, Wiltshire

'Works from the Collection', Yorkshire Sculpture Park, Wakefield

1994 'Sculpture Garden at Roche Court', New Art Centre, Wiltshire

'Back to the Future: Contemporary British Sculpture at Arundel Great Court', curated for Andersen Consulting by Art Guidelines Ltd

Tresors Fair, Singapore

1995 'Sculpture Garden at Roche Court', New Art Centre, Wiltshire

'Here and Now', Serpentine Gallery, London

'British Abstract Art Part 2: Sculpture', Flowers East, London

PUBLIC COLLECTIONS

Albright-Knox Art Gallery, Buffalo

Arts Council of Great Britain, London

Art Gallery of Ontario

British Council, London

British Government Art Collection

Contemporary Art Society, London

Dundee Museum and Art Gallery

Franklin P. Murphy Sculpture Garden, U.C.L.A., Los Angeles

Glasgow Museum and Art Gallery

Hirshhorn Museum and Sculpture Garden (Smithsonian Institute), Washington D.C.

Hull University Art Collection, Kingston-upon-Hull

McCrory Corporation, New York

Museum of Contemporary Art, Tehran

National Gallery of Art, Washington D.C.

Scottish National Gallery of Modern Art, Edinburgh

Städtisches Museum, Leverkusen

Swindon Museum and Art Gallery

Sydney Opera House

Tate Gallery, London

Victoria and Albert Museum, London

Westfälisches Landesmuseum, Munster

ILLUSTRATED BOOKS

Basho – The Records of a Weather Exposed Skeleton, Alistair McAlpine Publishing Ltd., London (limited edition) 1969

The Garden of Caresses, translated from the Arabic by Franz Toussaint, drawings by William Turnbull, Alistair McAlpine Publishing Ltd., London (limited edition) 1970

Der Wassermaler, by Helmut Heissenbuttel, aquatints by William Turnbull, published by Sybil Albers, Zurich (limited edition) 1976

BIBLIOGRAPHY

1950 Sylvester, David (intro.): William Turnbull (catalogue), Hanover Gallery, London

1952 Banham, Reyner: 'The Next Step', Art News and Review, 26 January

Ritchie, Andrew C: Sculpture of the Twentieth Century (catalogue), Museum of Modern Art, New York

1953 Waldberg, Isabelle: 'Essor de la Sculpture Anglaise', Numero, vol.5, nos.1 & 2, January/March

Alloway, Lawrence: 'Britain's New Iron Age', ARTnews, vol.52, June, pp.18–20, 68–70

1957 Alloway, Lawrence: 'Sculpture as Walls and Playgrounds', Architectural Design, January, p.26

Forge, Andrew: 'Round the London Galleries', The Listener, 10 October, p.547

Butcher, G.M: 'Alchemist Priest', Art News and Review, 12 October, p.10

Alloway, Lawrence (intro.): 'A Note on William Turnbull's Technique', William Turnbull (catalogue), Institute of Contemporary Arts, London

1958 Alloway, Lawrence: 'Marks and Signs', Ark, no.22, pp.37–41

1959 Seuphor, Michel: 'Le Choix d'un Critique', L'Œil, no.49, p.31

Alloway, Lawrence (intro.): European Art Today (catalogue), Walker Art Center, Minneapolis

1960 Coleman, Roger: 'William Turnbull', Art News and Review, 13 August

1960 (cont.)

Alloway, Lawrence: 'Avant Garde, London', Image, October

Seuphor, Michel: The Sculpture of this Century, publ. Wittenbourne, New York

Geidion-Welcker, Carola: Contemporary Sculpture, publ. Wittenbourne, New York

Alloway, Lawrence (intro.): 'Aphoristics and Monumental', William Turnbull (catalogue), Molton Gallery, London

Coleman, Roger (intro.): Situation (catalogue), R.B.A. Galleries, London

1961 Alloway, Lawrence: 'The Sculpture and Painting of William Turnbull', Art International, vol.5, no.1, 1 February, pp.46–52

Reichardt, Jasia: 'Bill Turnbull', Art News and Review, 22 April

'In Brancusi's Vein', The Times, 3 May

Langsner, Jules: 'The Way I See It', California, May 11

Crosby, Theo: 'International Union of Architects Congress Building, South Bank', (statement by William Turnbull), Architectural Design, November, pp.484–509

Alloway, Lawrence (intro.): 'Sculpture', William Turnbull (catalogue), Molton Gallery, London

Kulterman, Udo: Neue Malerei in England (catalogue), Städtisches Museum, Leverkusen, Germany

1962 Renfrew, Colin: 'The Tyranny of the Renaissance', Cambridge Review, 27 January, pp.219–23

Kulterman, Udo: Speculum Artis (Zürich), January/February

'LCC patronage of the arts', Art and Design, vol.XXXII, February

Kulterman, Udo: 'Neue Malerei in England', Das Kunstwerk, May, pp.2–9

Arnason, H. H (intro.): Modern Sculpture in the Joseph H. Hirshhorn Collection' (catalogue), Solomon R. Guggenheim Museum, New York, pp.58-59

1963 Hakanson, Joy: 'British Artist's Massive Sculptures Shown Here', Detroit News, December

1963 (cont.)

Driver, Morley: 'The Panorama of Centuries', Art in Detroit, December

Turnbull (catalogue), Marlborough-Gerson Gallery, New York

1964 Thieman, Eugen: 'William Turnbull', Das Kunstwerk, no.8/xvii, February, pp.7-23

Alloway, Lawrence (intro.): Guggenheim International (catalogue), Solomon R. Guggenheim Museum, New York

Read, Herbert: A Concise History of Modern Sculpture, publ. Thames & Hudson, London

International Directory of Contemporary Art, publ. Editoriale Metro, Milan

1965 Rudlinger, Arnold: Signale (catalogue), Kunsthalle, Basel

Baro, Gene (intro.): 'Paintings', William Turnbull (catalogue), Bennington College, Vermont

1966 Baro, Gene: 'A Changed Englishman, William Turnbull', Art in America, vol.54, March/April, pp.102–03

Langsner, Jules (intro.): 'Sculpture and Painting', William Turnbull (catalogue), Pavilion Gallery, Balboa, California

Baro, Gene: 'Turnbull's Nudes', London Magazine, September, pp.39–43

Baro, Gene: 'British Sculpture: The Developing Scene', Studio International, October, pp.171–82

1967 Russell, J: 'Down to the Bones', The Sunday Times, 16 April

Wolfram, E: 'Profile of Turnbull', Art News and Review, April, p.113

Huberman, B: 'La Aventura Artistica de William Turnbull', La Voz del Interior (Buenos Aires)

Reichhardt, Jasia: 'William Turnbull', Architectural Design, May, p.205

Whitford, Frank: 'The Paintings of William Turnbull', Studio, April, pp.202–04

Bowness, Alan: 'William Turnbull', IX Bienal Saõ Paolo (catalogue), British Council

1968 Sculpture 1967–68 (catalogue), Waddington Galleries, London

1970 Lynton, Norbert: 'Waddington: Minimal Art', The Guardian, 25 March

1971 Morphet, Richard: William Turnbull (catalogue), Alistair McAlpine Gift, Tate Gallery, London, pp.106–21

1972 Tate Gallery Acquisitions 1970–72, Tate Gallery Publications, London, pp.197–98

1973 Cohen, Bernard: 'William Turnbull – Painter and Sculptor', Studio International, vol.186, July/August, pp.9–16

Morphet, Richard (intro.): William Turnbull, Sculpture and Painting (catalogue), Tate Gallery, London

Oille, Jennifer: 'William Turnbull', Arts Review, vol.XXV, no.17, August

McNay, Michael: 'More or Less', Manchester Guardian, 18 August

Gaunt, William: 'William Turnbull', The Times, 22 August

Shepherd, Michael: 'Matter of Form', The Sunday Telegraph, 9 September

Hilton, Tim: 'The Scot who went to Paris', The Observer, 9 September

Whitford, Frank: 'Presbyterianischer Zen', Kunstforum, October, pp.205–10

1974 Feaver, William: 'William Turnbull', Art International, September, vol.XVIII, no.7, pp.28–32

Morphet, Richard (intro.): Recent Paintings, Sculptures and Prints by William Turnbull (catalogue), Scottish Arts Council Gallery, Edinburgh

Kudielka, Robert (intro.): 'Bilder', William Turnbull (catalogue), Galerie Muller, Stuttgart

1976 Wright, Frederick S: The Potent Image, publ. MacWilliam, pp.550–51

1977 Shone, Richard: The Century of Change: British Painting Since 1900, Phaidon Press, Oxford

1978 Burn, Guy: 'William Turnbull at Waddington & Tooth', Art Review, July

1978 (cont.)

William Turnbull: Drawings (catalogue), Waddington & Tooth Galleries, London

1979 Cohen, Bernard: 'William Turnbull – Painter and Sculptor', Decade (Boston), February, pp.30–38

Wilson, Simon: British Art, publ. Bodley Head, London

1981 Burr, James: 'Sculptural Intelligence', Apollo, March

Collier, Caroline: 'The Eternal Now', Arts Review, 13 March

Vaizey, Marina: 'William Turnbull', The Sunday Times, 15 March

Glaves-Smith, John: 'Turnbull', Art Monthly, no.45, April

William Turnbull (catalogue), Waddington Galleries, London

1982 Kramer, Hilton: 'William Turnbull', The New York Times, 8 January

Duncan, Stephen: 'Tension and Vitality, Figuration: Sculpture of the Fifties', Artscribe, no.35, June, pp.50–53

1983 William Turnbull (catalogue), Galerie Kutter, Luxembourg

1984 Ngui, Caroline: 'Sculpture with a Presence', The Straits Times, 19 September

Yu, Grace: 'Of subtle bronzes and cool stones', Business Times (Singapore), 24 September

Bevan, Roger (intro.): Kim Lim and William Turnbull (catalogue), National Museum of Singapore

Strachan, W. J.: Sutton Manor: permanent exhibition of XXth century sculpture, Sutton Manor Arts Centre

1985 Johnstone, Mog: 'William Turnbull' (review), Time Out, 5–11 December

William Turnbull (catalogue), Waddington Galleries, London

1986 Gooding, Mel: 'William Turnbull; Jock McFayden, Julian Trevelyan', Art Monthly, no.93, pp.16–17

Johnstone, Mog: 'William Turnbull', Artline, vol.3, no.1

1986 (cont.)

Massey, Anne: 'Pop at the I.C.A.', Art and Artists (UK), no.236, May, pp.11–14

Heartney, Eleanor: 'William Turnbull at Dintenfass', Art in America, May

H.S: 'William Turnbull', ARTnews, New York

1987 Massey, Anne: 'The Independent Group: towards a redefinition', Burlington Magazine, vol.129, no.1009, pp.232–42

Beaumont, Mary Rose: 'William Turnbull', Arts Review, 6 November, p.766

Russell, John: 'William Turnbull', The New York Times, 17 November

Taylor, John Russell: 'Shape of Things to Come', The Times, 17 November

Garlake, Margaret: 'Turnbull, Kestelman, Hyslop, McAleer', Art Monthly, December 1987/January 1988, pp.25–26

Bevan, Roger (intro.): William Turnbull (catalogue), Waddington Galleries, London

1988 Thomas, Mona: 'La sculpture anglaise', Beaux Arts, November, no.62, p.106

Curtis, Penelope: Modern British Sculpture from the Collection, Tate Gallery, Liverpool, pp.79, 89–90

Ollier, Bridget: 'La Sculpture anglaise prend aimant en Normandie', Libération

1989 Dobbels, Daniel: 'La Croisade des Anglais', Libération, 19 April

Wilson, Simon: Tate Gallery: An Illustrated Companion, Tate Gallery Publications, London

Curtis, Penelope: Patronage & Practice: Sculpture on Merseyside, Tate Gallery, Liverpool

1990 Morphet, Richard (intro.): Sculpture in the Close, Jesus College, Cambridge

Renfrew, Colin: 'The Sculptures of William Turnbull', Sculpture in the Close, Jesus College, Cambridge

1990 (cont.)

Robbins, David: The Independent Group: Postwar Britain and the Aesthetics of Plenty, MIT Press, Cambridge, Massachusetts, and London

1991 Phelps, Edward: 'Sculpture by the Spire', Arts Review, vol.XLIII, no.19, 20 September, p.467

Pearson, Fiona (ed.): Virtue and Vision, Sculpture and Scotland 1540–1990 (catalogue), National Galleries of Scotland

William Turnbull (catalogue), Waddington Galleries, London

Searle, Adrian: 'William Turnbull; Waddington's', Time Out, 9–16 October

Livingstone, Marco: Pop Art (catalogue), Royal Academy of Arts, London, p.147

1992 Ready, Steady, Go: Painting of the Sixties from the Arts Council Collection (catalogue), Arts Council & South Bank Centre publication

Sculpture (catalogue), Waddington Galleries, London

Le Cri et La Raison (catalogue), L'espace de l'art concret, Château de Mouans, Sartoux, Côtes d'Azur

William Turnbull (catalogue), Galeria Freites, Caracas

William Turnbull: New Sculpture (catalogue), Galerie Michael Haas, Berlin

New Beginnings: postwar British art from the collection of Ken Powell (catalogue), Scottish National Gallery of Modern Art, Edinburgh

1995 Kent, Sarah: 'British Sculpture: A thumbnail sketch', Here and Now (exhibition guide), Serpentine Gallery, London

Robertson, Bryan (intro.): British Abstract Art Part 2: Sculpture (catalogue), Flowers East, London